USING COGNITIVE APPROACHES WITH THE SERIOUSLY MENTALLY ILL

Dialogue Across the Barrier

Barbara A. Olevitch

Foreword by Albert Ellis

Westport, Connecticut
London

Library of Congress Cataloging-in-Publication Data

Olevitch, Barbara A.
    Using cognitive approaches with the seriously mentally ill : dialogue
across the barrier / Barbara A. Olevitch ; foreword by Albert Ellis.
        p.   cm.
    Includes bibliographical references and index.
    ISBN 0–275–95244–4 (alk. paper)
    1. Psychoses—Treatment. 2. Cognitive therapy. 3. Rational-
emotive psychotherapy. 4. Mentally ill — Rehabilitation.
    I. Ellis, Albert. II. Title.
    RC512.037   1995
    616.89'14—dc20   95–6348

British Library Cataloguing in Publication Data is available.

Library of Congress Catalog Card Number: 95–6348
ISBN: 0–275–95244–4

First published in 1995

Praeger Publishers, 88 Post Road West, Westport, CT 06881
An imprint of Greenwood Publishing Group, Inc.

Printed in the United States of America

∞

The paper used in this book complies with the
Permanent Paper Standard issued by the National
Information Standards Organization (Z39.48–1984).

10 9 8 7 6 5 4 3 2 1

To some unknown young person hearing voices for the first time, and to the mental health workers whom he or she will soon meet.

Contents

Foreword

This is an unusual and rare book because it deals with individuals who are diagnosed as being *really* mentally ill — including those who are schizophrenic and brain injured. It applies Rational Emotive Behavior Therapy (REBT) and other forms of Cognitive Behavior Therapy (CBT) to hospitalized and nonhospitalized psychotic individuals and shows how, in spite of their severe "emotional" problems, they can be fully accepted as worthwhile humans and can be active-directively taught how to lead less disturbed, more productive, and considerably happier lives.

Olevitch courageously marches in where most psychotherapists would greatly fear to tread. She patiently listens to exceptionally aberrated and often highly resistant patients, unconditionally accepts them with their cognitive, emotional, and behavioral deficiencies and handicaps, teaches them how to gain their own unconditional self-acceptance (what I have called USA), and gives them some remarkably useful skill training. No, she doesn't "cure" them. But, as many of them attest in this book, she often greatly helps them to becomes less demoralized and distraught and much more functional.

As the originator of REBT in 1955, I suppose that I can take some real credit for being one of the first users of cognitive behavior therapy with people with psychosis and with severe personality disorders, and I summarize some of the techniques I used with them in chapter 15, "The Treatment of Schizophrenia," in *Reason and Emotion in Psychotherapy* (Secaucus, NJ: Citadel, 1962). In rereading this and other early material

I wrote on treating people with mental illness, I am happy to see that I was well ahead of my times.

So, in the 1990s, is Barbara Olevitch. For she not only has treated mentally ill people successfully for a number of years but has devised some highly original methods of doing so. She uses REBT somewhat like I used it in the 1950s and 1960s, but she also has created a fascinating series of workshops to be used in residential care settings and she fully describes some of them in this book.

To make matters still better, Olevitch is a pioneer in creating and in field testing interactive videodisc simulation for the chronically mentally ill. The details that she gives in this book on her workshops and her videodisc simulation include extraordinary methods that, as far as I can see, no other psychologist-educator has presented. Her descriptions are invaluable for almost anyone working in the field of mental health.

In sum, this is a truly remarkable presentation of methods with which a highly active-directive, rational emotive behavioral practitioner can reach seriously disturbed individuals who are notoriously resistant to regular modes of psychotherapy. I congratulate Barbara Olevitch for her pioneering work in this field and sincerely hope that other mental health practitioners will learn from her innovative and brilliant work.

Albert Ellis

Acknowledgments

Without the fine clinical training experiences that I was fortunate enough to receive, I could not have written this book. Numerous supervisors were helpful, but I would like to single out Steven Starker, Jack Rakusin, Richard Munich, Elizabeth Brett, and Art Blank for special mention. Later in my career, workshops with Albert Ellis sponsored by the Institute for Rational Emotive Therapy in New York provided great clarification and inspiration.

Special thanks to Rod Vanderploeg, my partner in the development of the inpatient psychology workshops, and Lynn McLaughlin, our supervisor, who encouraged us to think beyond individual psychotherapy, and whose support was vital to our creative efforts. I also thank our interns and volunteers, whose enthusiastic participation made the workshops possible.

The "How to Get Out and Stay Out" disc would not have been possible without the foresight and support of James Hedlund of the Missouri Institute of Mental Health, who realized that interactive media in psychiatry were worth developing. It was also made possible through the creativity and extraordinary efforts of Brian Hagan, Susan Reidhead, and John Stalsworth, my production team, and the numerous volunteers who helped us.

The development of my thinking about my clinical experiences was greatly enhanced by the example of Jerome L. Singer, my graduate advisor, who set the process of psychotherapy into a broad theoretical context that enabled the integration of research and clinical experience. The discussions that I had with Joseph Zubin greatly enriched my under-standing of the social context of the chronic psychiatric patient.

I thank Albert Ellis, Esther Buddenhagen, Mark Edison, Lynn McLaughlin, Lea Singer, and my husband for reading earlier drafts of this manuscript and making comments that enabled me to improve it.

Most of all, I thank my patients for sharing their stories and their thoughts with me and for their feedback about what was helpful and what was not.

A final thank you goes to my family — to my mother and father who raised me in an atmosphere of truthfulness that helped me to develop whatever insight I have and to my husband and son for making all those little and not-so-little sacrifices that enabled me to finish this book.

General Introduction: Achieving Meaningful Communication with the Mentally Ill

I vividly remember how frightened I was before beginning training to work with seriously mentally ill patients. I spent considerable time trying to imagine what these patients would be like, but the only knowledge I had of them came from books that were highly theoretical. My mind was full of bewildering abstractions derived from these books — I was going to be talking to people who were "regressed," "out of touch with reality," "biochemically imbalanced," and who had difficulty with "cognitive filtering." They would all be taking medication, which would at least partially correct these problems. How could I communicate with them? What should I communicate with them about? I felt like I was entering an unfamiliar territory without a map.

I was fortunate to begin my work in a treatment program that had been organized by people who strongly believed in the capacity of the mentally ill to communicate and to recuperate. I was immensely relieved as soon as I attended my first group with the patients. To my great satisfaction they were having an animated discussion, and I was immediately able to understand what they were talking about. There was a young man who wanted a job and an older woman who was afraid to live alone. Even though their biochemical and cognitive handicaps created a barrier to communication, our groups were conducted in such a way that we were able to communicate across that barrier.

Many hospital staff members working with the mentally ill today have not been as fortunate in their training opportunities. Because of funding cutbacks, there are fewer and fewer special treatment programs with high staff-to-patient ratios where trainees can hear supervisors interacting successfully with the mentally ill and where the mentally ill get enough continuous attention for the trainees to witness obvious improvements.

We are now entering an era of new optimism about psychosocial treatment. Because of the successes of behaviorally-oriented social skills programs with the mentally ill, hospitals are being reorganized, and mental health workers are being called upon to organize structured group activities for seriously mentally ill patients for rehabilitation and skills training. Because of the pressure to create these new training activities and the difficulty of designing these activities there is a danger that activities that are not truly effective or that are perceived by hospital patients in a negative way may be quickly set into place (Turner, 1991).

Fortunately, there are now a few different kinds of materials, such as videotapes, manuals, and videodiscs, being designed and evaluated to help leaders organize groups for the seriously mentally ill (Liberman & Corrigan, 1993; Olevitch & Hagan, 1989, 1991). A recent book, *Cognitive-behavioral Therapy of Schizophrenia* (Kingdon & Turkington, 1994), provides enough good examples of ways of explaining important points to psychotic patients to give practitioners a head start in their efforts to communicate effectively.

The era of new optimism about the rehabilitation of the mentally ill can be sustained if we can soon evolve a wide variety of educational and rehabilitative experiences that are genuinely meaningful to the mentally ill. It is, therefore, with some sense of urgency that I have written this book, in which I share my experiences talking to and teaching the mentally ill. It is my hope that this record of my experiences and thoughts will make some contribution toward encouraging and enabling mental health workers to enter into a meaningful dialogue across the barrier with their psychotic patients. It is not, of course, a complete guide, because no single book can be, but it is my hope that others who have entered this area will also write about it and that together we will evolve more materials to inspire and guide those who wish to help the seriously mentally ill.

In Part I, the focus is on achieving the kind of one-to-one communication that helps to alleviate the desperation that individuals so often feel during hospitalization.

Parts II, III, and IV focus on preventive programs that can be offered on a regular basis to build up psychological strengths in patients who suffer from serious mental illnesses.

I

INDIVIDUAL SESSIONS

1

Introduction to Part I: Assisting the Patient's Thought Process

The following chapters give examples of how patients with serious symptoms and cognitive handicaps can be assisted in their ongoing effort to cope with the difficult circumstances of being mentally ill and to think productively enough to keep up with their current "workload" of everyday problems.

In the section that follows, I describe some of the individual therapy that I have done with psychotic patients. In the course of describing the paths that I took in talking to each patient, I sometimes describe the path that I did not take.

I find that, in the field of mental health, we have not only a written tradition (technical journals and books), but also an oral tradition. Often in the course of describing my therapy I find myself arguing against ideas from this oral tradition, mostly against negative, cynical, and discouraging ideas.

In the course of reading about how I set aside these negative ideas, some mental health workers might feel that I am treating some of their ideas lightly. I would like to say at the outset that I have not meant to criticize or put down the people who hold these ideas. I only mean to take these ideas out of the comfortable context of an oral tradition in which they are often repeated but rarely challenged and question them, I hope, in the scholarly tradition of open discussion.

This section on individual sessions with psychotic patients was written at an earlier time, when I still had reason to hope that there might be increasing interest in the topic of how to do cognitively oriented individual psychotherapy with psychotic patients. At the time that I wrote these vignettes, I already felt apologetic because they fell far short of classic case studies; the rapidly moving caseload in a modern hospital did not permit me to include the patients' long-term histories or outcomes. Little did I know that even the kind of short-term cognitive therapy that I was providing was becoming a luxury in an inpatient setting.

I was gradually evolving another concept of the purpose of the individual sessions that I had with patients. Instead of seeing the purpose of the session as being the execution of a procedure called therapy that was supposed to effect a permanent change in the patient, I began to see the sessions as, instead, what might be called a thinking-assist.

Imagine a volleyball game. Someone in the back row runs for a hard serve and hits it rapidly toward the net, almost high enough to make it over the net. The person in the front row reaches out and taps the ball just slightly, enabling it to go over the net. This is the kind of assistance that I have in mind. The brain of the patient is not functioning optimally. The patient is almost thinking in a manner that would be productive, but not quite. The therapist challenges a belief or two, adds a little information about the probable reactions of others, adds a little encouragement, and with this assistance, the patient is able to accomplish some productive thinking during the session.

Schizophrenia and other psychotic conditions create a mental handicap. As therapists, we do not reduce the patient's handicap; however, we can do several things.

1. We can teach the patient stress management, with the goal of decreasing the likelihood of relapse.
2. We can help the patient to cope with some of the special, painful circumstances of being mentally ill.
3. We can help the patient to keep up with his or her current "workload" of healthy problem solving.

The opportunity that I had to talk individually with psychotic patients was an invaluable education for me and provided the basis for the group workshops that I began to do later. I include the accounts of the individual sessions because the content reveals the nature of psychotic thinking and provides the reader with a basis for understanding psychotic concerns that come up in a group context. I also include them because I believe that there will always be some need for individual treatment. Some patients have complex ideas that simply cannot be handled in a group. Some are easily embarrassed and cannot share their own concerns in a group, although they can learn from what they hear about others. Therefore, individual sessions at critical times may always be a necessary adjunct to group educational sessions.

2

Some Rational Emotive Behavioral or Cognitive Tools for Working with the Seriously Mentally Ill

In spite of the severity of the presenting problems of many hospitalized patients, a therapist can provide emotional relief and needed instruction to a wide variety of hospital patients by remembering to focus on a few major categories of "irrational" thoughts.

Like many young psychologists, I explored a number of different psychotherapy approaches and learned something valuable from each one. The approach that ultimately gave me the most practical day-to-day guidance working with psychotic patients on a busy inpatient ward was Albert Ellis's rational emotive behavior therapy (REBT) (Ellis, 1993; Ellis & Harper, 1975). Ellis points out that psychotherapy for psychotic patients is "ameliorative" rather than "curative" (1962, p. 287). Given this limitation, he states that his therapy "is one of the very best methods of choice in treating psychotics. It presents a view of life and a cognitive-emotive approach to reality that is unusually clear, understandable, and teachable" (p. 286).

According to Ellis, it is not the events that happen to a person, but his or her beliefs about the events, that lead to a feeling of despair. Ellis calls certain thoughts "irrational." These thoughts cause the individual to suffer from unnecessarily painful emotions, such as anger and depression. By learning to talk themselves out of these irrational beliefs, people can reduce their emotional suffering. Aaron Beck has also made major contributions to this type of therapy, which he calls "cognitive therapy" (see especially Thase & Beck, 1993; Scott, Byers, & Turkington, 1993).

By highlighting a few major categories of irrational thoughts, Ellis's theory helped me to organize my work in an environment that was often potentially chaotic but that required me to act quickly and with a clear focus.

In a hospital, the therapist must remember to focus on the patient's thoughts because the patient may report a series of events that are so dangerous or dramatic the therapist may completely forget to ask what the patient is thinking about those events. However, if the therapist is not distracted by the enormity of the reported events or by the severity of the patient's psychiatric diagnosis and directs the attention of the patient toward his or her thoughts, the therapist may find they are classic irrational thoughts described by Ellis. The therapist then knows how to begin working with the patient. The therapist cannot cure the patient's biochemical disorder, and the patient may still have psychiatric symptoms in spite of medication, but the therapist can aim at alleviating some unnecessary misery.

Knowing just a few major categories of irrational statements provided me with guidance in a number of different clinical situations.

1. I am a _____(self-reproachful noun).
2. I need _____, I have to _____.
3. I should _____, they should _____.
4. I can't stand it.

With experience, I was able to extend the use of these few categories into a repertoire of REBT or cognitive interventions applying to hospitalized patients.

I AM A SUCH-AND-SUCH

When a patient is admitted to a hospital in a suicidal state, the therapist has a critical opportunity. The therapist is going to hear the thoughts that are closely connected with the patient's deepest feelings of despair. If the therapist can give the patient some tools for overcoming these thoughts, the patient can be strengthened.

In October a middle-aged man was admitted to the hospital. He told me that he had been planning to kill himself. He had realized that the Christmas season was coming, and, because of his unemployment, he would be unable to buy presents for his children. He felt that he couldn't face Christmas without having presents for his children, so he had been planning to jump off a bridge. He thought that his wife would do fine without him — she would meet somebody else — but it occurred to him that, without him, the children would lead a miserable life with no one to take care of them. He thought that he ought to get a gun and kill them first before he jumped off the bridge.

I asked what his thoughts were about having no presents for the children.

"I am a failure," he answered.

"Tell me," I asked, gently, "is there really such a thing as being a complete failure?"

He looked slightly startled. His eyes, which had previously been dull, showed a flicker of interest, but he hesitated.

"Do you understand what I mean?" I asked.

"Yes," he said. "Sometimes a person messes things up pretty bad, but they're not a failure."

"Tell me," I asked, "are there really two kinds of people, some who just mess things up sometimes and some others who are really complete failures and can't do anything but mess things up?"

"No," he said. "I know what you mean. People have hard times, but they don't have to last forever."

He looked a little surprised and encouraged. He had made a good beginning in the conversation, having found his way out of the seductive logic of the irrational statement underlying much depression: I am a _____ (some self-reproach, in his case, "failure"). He was now ready to realize that his own well-being was much more important to his children than any presents that he could buy them. The situation was still the same, but it had lost its sting. He was ready to begin a process of recuperation, during which his family would rally around him, glad to see him looking animated again.

Because entering a psychiatric hospital is an act of despair, it is not surprising that many hospitalized patients have drawn similar fatalistic conclusions about themselves and continue to draw these conclusions every day about small events. Just because a patient is chronically schizophrenic and has convinced himself or herself, and perhaps others, that he or she is one of the "failures," the "losers" that people sometimes talk about, there is no reason why he or she cannot benefit from this same kind of discussion of the essential nature of the self-reproach.

A young woman diagnosed as a schizophrenic entered my office for a session. She looked at me imploringly and said as she sat down, "Someone just asked me for a cigarette. I should have said 'no.' I'm a fool. I never learn. I'm all screwed up."

I was ready with my questions.

"Are there really some people who never learn at all?" I asked.

She responded positively to this kind of discussion, saying, "This is really helping me."

The line of questioning that I have suggested here is not the reaction that self-reproachful people typically get from other people. Usually, a friend, acquaintance, relative, or therapist will seek to console someone who is self-reproachful by convincing them that the self-reproach isn't true. They might remind the person who says he is a "failure" of something that he did well, or remind the person who says, "I never learn" that she has a college degree. This approach is what Albert Ellis calls the "inelegant solution" to the problem. The reason this method of solution is not elegant is that, although the despairing person may be temporarily persuaded that he is not at this moment a "failure" or a "person who never learns," he still believes in the existence of "failures" and "people who never learn." Therefore, the possibility of becoming such a person or discovering conclusive evidence that he is such a person is still agonizingly open.

The elegant solution closes this possibility. Having examined a self-reproach and having concluded that it is based upon an exaggeration, with practice a person possesses a tool to keep himself from taking this self-reproach quite so seriously in the future. If he articulates this reproach to himself again, he may remind himself that it is an exaggeration. He may still be disappointed with himself, but not in despair.

I NEED

In his books on rational emotive behavior therapy, Albert Ellis reminds us that there is only a small list of things necessary for life — food, air, water, shelter (some of my patients have pointed out that for some people, medication is also on this list). Unfortunately, though, people do not enjoy the fact that we actually need so little. Without realizing it, they add many items to their own personal list of needs, items that are not really necessary for life — like career success, the esteem of others, etc. This tendency to believe that they need all these things, which are actually in the category of wants rather than needs, can cause a person who is disappointed in one of his or her goals to panic, reacting emotionally to a social disappointment as if it were a life-and-death matter.

Someone who is disappointed in something that he knows was just a want feels sad and frustrated but not paralyzed. He can rethink his situation, modify his goal, modify his strategies, and become reenergized.

However, someone who believes that what he missed out on was a need can feel paralyzed. Because he feels that he can proceed no further without it, he is vulnerable to becoming absorbed in seeking to place blame for his plight.

Unfortunately, the popularization and widespread misunderstanding of the process of psychotherapy has actually convinced some people to extend rather than shorten their list of perceived needs. People with psychiatric problems that affect their thinking often take ideas from the popular culture more seriously than mentally healthy people do. I have encountered patients who believe that they have to have a loving family, the support of their parents, a trauma-free childhood, and, if not, years of therapy with an understanding, stable therapist who forms a relationship with them to somehow make up for what they missed.

Unfortunately, the hospitals have many young people for whom the items on this extended list are unattainable. Raised in a series of foster homes, abandoned or perhaps abused multiple times, these young people have often already sought psychological help in the public hospitals and have been disappointed because they could not get as much therapy as they thought necessary.

For this group, I was able to muster the courage to apply Albert Ellis's ideas in undiluted form — what I call "hard-core REBT." The essence of this philosophy states, "you don't need to have had a happy childhood. What is hurting you now is not the fact that you had the unhappy childhood, but some of the thoughts about the unhappy childhood that you have now. In order to help you feel better, we can talk about examples from right now of what bothers you and how you think about it. Anything that helps you learn about your own thoughts and how they affect your feelings will help you."

These ideas can provide some relief to the patient. Imagine the burden of believing you needed a kind of therapeutic relationship that no one had the time to provide. Imagine the relief of finding out that there were things you could learn that would help you change some negative emotions and behavior and that you could accumulate more and more self-knowledge step by step, learning from different people and different situations.

The irrational statements that Ellis discovered can trigger intense emotions. Changing these statements changes the nature of the emotions elicited. When someone thinks, "I needed supportive parents," she feels stunted and possibly enraged. But when she thinks "it would have been nice if I had supportive parents," she feels sad, not crippled. She can begin a search for supportive friends and mentors.

SHOULD

I am speaking to a young man who has lost a series of jobs for arguing with his supervisors and has angered both patients and staff on the ward by telling them what to do and threatening them. He makes a stern face and points his finger at me in a scolding gesture, telling me what someone did and how they "shouldn't" have done it. He begins to get angrier and angrier as he is captivated by his own logic.

I smile and say to him playfully, "Remember what I said about not pointing your finger at me?"

His whole demeanor changes. The stern expression disappears entirely from his face. He looks amused and grateful. He rolls his eyes as if to say, "oops, I forgot." With his scolding finger still suspended in the air, he reaches over with his other hand and, in an exaggerated comical manner, bends the suspended finger in such a way that the knuckle cracks, making him laugh.

The message of all psychotherapies is that we sometimes take our own emotions too seriously. Generated by habit in a sequence of neural patterns, emotions can be interrupted if we learn how to do so. By questioning the "should" or holding back a scolding finger, a painful and possibly dangerous episode of "righteous" wrath can often be averted.

I CAN'T STAND IT

A patient who is in the process of recovering from a serious episode of mental illness is asked how it began. Her reply makes it clear that this episode had not been precipitated by the sorts of major life transitions that one might expect to elevate stress — a death, a divorce, or loss of a job or a friend. Instead, there was an unfortunate, simultaneous occurrence of numerous everyday problems.

"Do you remember what you were thinking that day, when your car broke down and your pipes froze and your telephone was out of order?"

"Yes, I do remember. I kept thinking 'I can't stand it!' I just didn't know what to do!"

The thought "I can't stand it" can transform a feeling of being annoyed and overwhelmed into a feeling of panic and unreality. Having made this statement to herself, an individual sometimes feels justified in taking actions that do not make sense. In some people the statement creates a justification for the suspension of logical thought and the beginning of a purely emotional reaction, which can lead anywhere.

Questioning this statement can alleviate the patient's panic. However uncomfortable the situation was, the patient actually did tolerate it, and she feels better realizing that she underestimated her own strength. The collapse that she anticipated was more imaginary than real. Looking out for this confusing statement can help patients to maintain better judgment in crisis situations.

3

Delusions

This chapter explains how to respectfully go over the steps in a delusional patient's thinking. It gives an example of a man who thought that his food was being poisoned and a woman who thought someone was trying to murder her.

There are certain statements that circulate widely whose origins no one seems to know, whose meaning is unclear, and whose validity has never been tested. One of these is, "never argue with a psychotic patient about his or her delusions."

As a young inpatient therapist, I had the good fortune to run into a patient who encouraged me to question this warning. Mr. H was an appealing, middle-aged man who was admitted to the hospital during a family crisis. He improved very rapidly, almost before we could mobilize ourselves to help him, and he spent his sessions with me going over some of the ways in which he could help himself to accept his situation philosophically. He experienced a feeling of strength and enthusiasm that he was eager to share, as many people do when they overcome a crisis. I was deeply impressed by what he said about his past treatment.

"Don't believe it when they tell you not to argue with the patient," he confided. "Dr. J really helped me. I argued back with him at the time, but much later on I thought about what he said." Mr. H's record corroborated that he had at one time been hospitalized for several years with religious delusions and had required treatment on a locked ward. What intrigued me particularly about his story was the idea that Dr. J might never have known that his arguments had been helpful.

There are several reasons why many therapists do not try to influence patients' delusional beliefs directly. They believe that it isn't nice to argue with the patient, and it doesn't do any good. To many polite people, the term "argue" has a negative connotation. The term "argument" can be used in a different way, however. Rather than referring to a conceptual struggle between two people, it can refer to the steps in a logical thought process. Thus, in order to understand why someone reached a certain scientific or mathematical conclusion, you might ask, "What are the steps in your argument?" This is respectful. You would not ask such a question if you did not care about the details of his thought process. Perhaps you ask it because you believe that the person has good judgment and you are open to being persuaded by him. It also implies that you are willing to spend the amount of time with him that it would take to hear and understand something that might be complicated.

Asking the patient how she arrived at a certain conclusion can be done in a way that makes the patient feel that you are interested in her. After all, the sequence of thoughts and experiences that convinced the patient of her conclusion is one of her life experiences, possibly one of her most treasured life experiences.

Perhaps some therapists think it is not supportive to question the patient on her delusions because they feel that, because the patient's ideas are mistaken, the patient will be embarrassed. There are several procedures that can be followed to minimize the patient's discomfort. First, *begin your interaction with the patient as soon as possible rather than letting the patient ramble.* If you disagree with the very first thing the patient says and then listen politely while she draws a series of conclusions from her first statement, there is a greater risk that when you finally do speak, the patient will feel embarrassed. By then the patient may have said more that is mistaken. Not only that, but the patient will be less open to examining her thought process because, by then, she is more likely to be carried away by her own rhetoric.

Beginning your interaction with the patient sooner will avoid these problems. Perhaps you feel that by questioning, you would be interrupting the patient. The kind of interruption that is considered rude in ordinary conversation occurs because the person who interrupts is not listening to the speaker. I am suggesting a different kind of interruption, the kind that occurs because you *are* listening.

A psychotic person can and often does overwhelm the information processing capacity of anyone who listens to her passively. There is a term called "active listening;" in the case of psychotic patients, we might want to coin a new term, "hyperactive listening." They experience it as very supportive because it provides them with an opportunity to be understood. Receiving help in structuring their thought process is also good exercise and good modeling. The questions you ask them give them practice in questioning their own thought process as they go along. Lucidity does not come naturally. It is a skill based upon accumulated experience, which only accumulates if you keep asking yourself how you might be confusing the listener. Hearing the listener's questions is a good way to develop this skill.

What type of interaction would be preferable? How can the patient be guided along in a constructive direction? An important thing to remember when you hear a statement that appears to be unreasonable is to consider it as a conclusion. The unreasonable statement did not spring full-blown out of the patient's dopamine receptors like Athena from the head of Zeus. Just as smoke implies a fire, a conclusion implies premises. When the conclusion seems unreasonable, try to find out what the premises were. Do not seek more details about the conclusion or engage in a process that encourages the patient to elaborate the conclusion. Do not expect the patient to simply replace his conclusion without going over the premises and the argument.

If you can manage to get the patient to tell you the premises of his argument, you may be favorably surprised. They are likely not to be as absurd as the conclusion. You may find yourself on familiar ground as a therapist. The premises are very likely to be concerns about inadequacy. You are then engaged in a therapeutic dialogue in which you can use some of the same therapeutic skill that you use with nonpsychotic patients.

Mr. M is an example of a delusional patient. When I met him, he was a young, healthy looking man with a very loud, deep voice. He was already a chronic patient. He was angry and frightened, sputtering that someone had gotten into his refrigerator and put poison into his milk. His psychiatric record showed that he had entered the hospital many times with the same complaint.

I did not challenge his conclusion. To just promptly say, "No one is poisoning your milk" would be an assertion of superiority. That statement would imply that I am somehow the judge of what is possible and what is not possible, and that I can just tell what is true, which of course I cannot.

Sometimes mental health professionals become frustrated when patients will not accept our conclusions instead of theirs. They consider it poor judgment on the patient's part. However, it is not just psychotic patients who are stubborn about the results of their thinking processes. Just because their conclusions may be somewhat more absurd than ours does not mean that they are not just as attached to their conclusions. Suppose you had just worked out an arithmetic problem and you believed you had done it correctly. How would you feel if someone challenged your answer and expected you to change your mind? Wouldn't it be a strength not to be so easily influenced? Asch showed that a surprisingly large percentage of people will go along with the majority opinion even if it directly contradicts what they see with their own eyes (Hilgard, Atkinson, & Atkinson, 1975). Perhaps the psychotic person you are talking to doesn't share this common flaw of the average personality, or at least is not manifesting it at that moment. In the case of the arithmetic example, a feeling of conviction in the correctness of the other person's answer can only be achieved by going over each step of the calculation. If I believe for some reason that the other person is smarter than I am or better at math, I can assume that their answer must be correct even though I don't understand why. This is not, however, the same as believing that the new answer is correct independent of whose answer it is. I might also pretend to accept the other answer because I don't want to think about it any more. Accepting the answer because of the authority of the other person or because I don't want to think are not as desirable as accepting the new answer because I now understand it. If the other person can show me where I made my mistake, then I alter all the subsequent steps, and the other's answer becomes my answer.

The process of revising a sequence of thoughts does not have to be a painful experience for the person who made the mistake. It can be fun to be persuaded to see things a new way, especially if the new way is less confusing and allows the patient to be more in agreement with other people than before. But this process is usually very hard work for the person who has to do the persuasion, because he has to follow a much more tortuous, confusing way of thinking than he is accustomed to.

In spite of the difficulty of going over erroneous thought processes in detail, even science teachers are finding that unless this is done, students do not learn well. Researchers have found that students have "naive theories" of physics and other sciences that persist unless they are dealt with directly by the instructor (Chinn & Brewer, 1993). Psychotic thought processes are naive theories about what accounts for success, failure, pain, and well-being.

I did not ask Mr. M to elaborate his conclusion. I did not ask how anyone could get into his refrigerator or how often they came, or why they would want to do this to him. I wouldn't want to ask him a question he had never thought of before and actually cause him to elaborate the delusion further.

I did ask Mr. M what made him think that his milk was being tampered with. When he indicated that this had happened before and it was simply happening again, I asked him to tell me about what was going on the first time he came to this conclusion. He stated that this had started when he was in the military. I asked him what it was about his sensations, thoughts, or behavior that led him to conclude that he had been poisoned. He stated that he had begun doing poorly in his training courses and, rather than believe that he was "stupid," he concluded that his functioning had been interfered with by another party.

From that point on, I felt that I was on solid ground. Whatever Mr. M's other inadequacies, whatever his vulnerability to psychotic decompensation, whatever his level of intellectual functioning, I knew what to do to get him started on reducing his fear and shame regarding the possibility of what he was calling "stupidity." Whatever his other problems, I could hope that he would be a little stronger as a result of our session.

The diagram in Figure 1 illustrates the way in which I imagine the possible pathways of the patient's thought process when interacting with a patient like Mr. M. The patient encounters a problem, major or minor. If the patient concludes, "I'm a failure," (or "dependent," "helpless," or "stupid," and so on) there is literally no further logical conclusion that he can draw that is not essentially unproductive and self-defeating. However, if he avoids this kind of negative conclusion, there are literally thousands of productive ways to conceptualize and progress from his initial problem.

I entered directly into a discussion of "stupidity" and what it is. After a few questions that directed his attention away from himself and toward examining what he meant by "stupidity," he was easily able to conclude the following:

1. Just because a person fails one subject, doesn't mean that his mind is incapable of learning anything or that he can't achieve things or have a happy life.

2. Even if he were, in fact, of low intelligence, he might not need to give up on doing anything. He might have to study the same material longer than normal people, but he might be able to catch on if he kept trying. In this context, "stupidity" is seen as a nuisance and an obstacle, but not as a reason for panic.

FIGURE 1
Thought Processes upon Encountering a Problem

SELF-DEFEATING THOUGHTS   PRODUCTIVE THOUGHTS

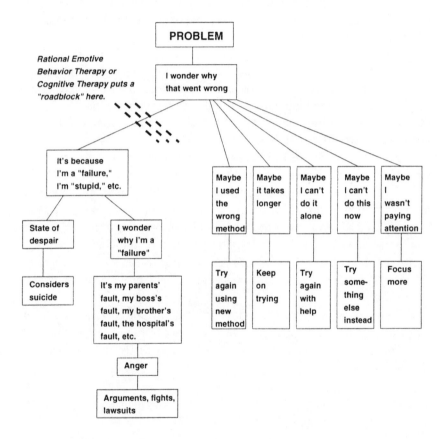

3. Even if he remained unable to understand many things, he would not need to be ashamed of this. This would be more of a problem for those around him than for himself.

I could almost see Mr. M relax visibly as soon as we entered this discussion. By treating the possibility of low intelligence as a handicap to his productive activities that he could cope with on an everyday basis just as other people cope with other obstacles, we gave him almost immediate relief from a large emotional burden — the burden of believing that what he was calling "stupidity" was a condition that would exclude him forever from practical activities.

The patient's panic comes from an idea that seems to be believed by many people in their weaker moments. We can call this idea the myth of the subhuman class. It consists of the doctrine that there are two types of people, normal and subhuman, and that each person belongs forever in one of these two categories.

According to this myth, the subhuman class is not merely disabled; its members are considered to be morally loathsome and blameworthy. To comprehend the emotion associated with this idea of a group of subhumans, think of the way teenagers feel about "creeps" or "nerds." Life experiences are seen, from this point of view, not in terms of their consequences or in terms of what might be learned from them, but, instead, as signs of whether one is in the subhuman category or not. The patient is distressed by a panicky thought that he has never fully examined that he may be a member of this subhuman class. He has attempted many times to test himself, hoping to prove that he does not have this hopelessly low status, but he has never succeeded in convincing himself. It is still an open topic that preoccupies him, saps his energy, and fills him with anxiety.

It is important for the therapist to understand that, if indeed there were a subhuman class, and if indeed there were some ambiguity about whether a person belonged to it, it would make sense for these people to give this all-absorbing question top priority in their mental life because there would be no point to wasting their efforts trying to act normal if in fact they are in a separate subhuman category. Only by directly challenging the idea that there is such a division can the therapist remove the foundation that is supporting all of the patient's urgent ruminations.

Every patient who is fearful of being a member of such a subhuman class has a different way of describing it. For example, one patient, in a very negative tone of voice, would refer to "people who depend on others." In each case, the therapist can ask questions that challenge the absoluteness and the irrevocability of the separation that the patient is making. Isn't it true, the therapist can ask, that many people have to rely on others for certain periods in their lives? Isn't it true that by relying on others for a while, some people become even stronger than they would have been? Isn't it true that some people who are supported by their families make a considerable contribution to the family that is informal, for example, doing chores, shopping, visiting the sick? Isn't it true that some people who are now receiving help from others were helpful to others in the past when they were stronger?

The patient often knows exactly what the therapist is talking about. The disputation of the irrational beliefs is never entirely new to the patient, no matter how disturbed he is. He recognizes the therapist's arguments against the idea that there is such a thing as a person totally engulfed by a weakness. A patient will often say, "Oh yes, I used to think that way . . . back when I felt better." When he is able to refresh his grasp on these already familiar ideas — that the myth of the subhuman class isn't true, and that he could live with the flaws he has been fearing — he sometimes looks as if he had been reunited with a trusted old friend.

The sooner the therapist can plunge into a discussion of this basic myth of the subhuman class, often by simply asking, "is there really such a thing as . . . a 'failure,' a 'total ignoramus,' and so on," the sooner the patient can experience the refreshing effect of this challenge. Many therapists hesitate, as if it were rude to suggest that something a person mentions may not exist. The therapist may feel awkward, but only by trying this maneuver can the therapist verify for himself the benefit the patient experiences. The patient who is suffering because of the myth of the subhuman class is already thinking at an abstract level. By clearly articulating the issue, the therapist gives the patient the opportunity to communicate and to challenge these troublesome thoughts.

Mr. M seemed to enjoy our discussion, and he calmed down sufficiently to leave the hospital soon afterward. Our team had been trying for a long time to place him in a supervised facility where he could get vocational rehabilitation, but he had always left the hospital before the placement could be arranged. Soon after his discharge he came back to the hospital, but this time he was not delusional. He had gone to his local mental health center and had been given a pamphlet to read about the symptoms of schizophrenia. When he had seen the fear of being poisoned listed in print as a problem that a lot of people had, he finally had the insight that what he was experiencing was a symptom. He decided that he did need special help and came back to work on his placement. I always wondered whether our conversations had helped to prepare him for the experience he had when he read the pamphlet. Was he more ready to accept himself as having a disability because this no longer had a connotation of being irreparably subhuman? A therapist never knows for sure.

In thinking about the case, I was glad that I immediately began talking to Mr. M about his concept of stupidity and did not defer this discussion until more objective evaluative data regarding his intelligence was available. I knew, because of his military experience, that retardation was not a possibility. If I had deferred further discussion with Mr. M while waiting for test results, I might have lost an opportunity. Given the brevity of most inpatient hospitalizations, by the time the tests were scored, the patient might have been ready to leave. Any topic that is deferred in the first interview might never be discussed again. The most critical point for Mr. M was not whether he could have passed certain courses or not, but whether it would have been a catastrophe if he could not.

I did not feel that I needed an intellectual assessment of Mr. M before I could proceed with cognitive therapy. I have encountered some therapists in training who were not drawn to cognitive therapy because they believed that a client has to be highly intelligent to benefit from it and that this therapy somehow makes the patient more intellectual than they already are. This is not the case. The theory of rational emotive behavior therapy (REBT) does not state that people would be better off if they thought more. In fact, of all the therapies, it idealizes the intellect the least. In REBT, the thought process is seen to be the source of the patient's difficulties. Patients are feeling excessive negative feelings because of the way in which they have been thinking. Even a client with an intellectual level that is below average is not exempt from this process. Clients carrying diagnoses of borderline intelligence or mild retardation can often participate in REBT, and they are capable of insight into their emotional processes. They can understand that thinking "I'm no good" makes them feel sad, and they are sometimes eloquent in their insights.

The possibility that Mr. M's poor performance was attributable to the developing symptoms of schizophrenia also did not make me feel that REBT was inappropriate. If someone is fighting a tendency to become psychotic, then he must learn to be even more rational than the average person. For example, suppose an individual with a tendency to become psychotic stays up late studying for an exam or worrying about it, and she starts feeling a bit confused. If she starts to say to herself, "here I go again; I'm just a crazy person. I can't do anything any more without cracking up," I hypothesize that this line of thinking might induce panic and trigger further biochemical abnormalities. But suppose that after a course of cognitive therapy, she learns to say to herself, "Maybe I'll flunk but it's not the end of the world. Maybe I get a little confused sometimes but nobody's perfect. I'll never be at the top of the class but I can still enjoy myself anyway." This soothing chain of thoughts may have the power to avert panic and possibly minimize further biochemical deviations and confusion.

The idea that the patient has a biochemical abnormality can cause a therapist to become easily discouraged when trying to teach stress management to a psychotic person. I remind myself frequently that there are other states besides psychosis that cause biochemical changes and that these changes do not make it impossible to communicate. When people are fatigued, their brains are probably in a different biochemical state than when they are well rested. However, it is possible to communicate with a fatigued person. It may not be possible to convey everything, but a reasonable conversation can be held and retained despite the effects of fatigue. The biochemical abnormality of the psychotic patient may be considered in a similar light. Perhaps the same person without the psychosis may have been much easier to work with and may have achieved higher levels of understanding and more successful stress management, but even with a psychosis, the human mind is an instrument capable of learning. There is no need for despair on the part of the therapist.

If my conversation was in vain, have I unnecessarily disturbed the patient? I am very aware of this possibility and try not to push the patients where they don't want to go. I watch the patients' facial expressions very carefully. Often, when I question them, they seem pleased or amused. I look for their faces to become more animated, to lose that flat look. If a topic makes them seem more animated and pleased, I pursue it further. One woman, commenting on a session in which we had talked about her delusion, said, "That was interesting. That was different. You really went into depth." Every so often, the patient seems amused at my expense, and echoes the sentiments of those who worry about cost-effectiveness. He or she asks, "Why are you spending so much time with me? You can't help me," but seems pleased that I am trying.

I strongly believe that a session of REBT does not need to be aversive. Some people believe that the content of therapy is essentially painful because the patient has to deal with issues that he has been avoiding. In the case of Mr. M, he did not have to deal with any bad news at all. He had a concern that he might be a hopelessly deficient person. This made him angry because he had not always been hopelessly deficient and felt it must be somebody's fault. If someone encounters a minor obstacle, such as a fallen tree lying across his path, he does not rant and rave inwardly about how the tree got there, he simply steps over it and goes on. If, however, he encounters a major obstacle that he cannot bypass, such as becoming hopelessly deficient in the abilities necessary to engage in normal activities, it would be only natural to spend a large amount of time bemoaning the circumstances that led to this situation and raging at anyone who might have been responsible. By discussing whether Mr. M was indeed hopelessly deficient, we relieved him of the necessity to explain how this came about. He then had less reason to follow the path of trying to find a villain and more reason to veer toward trying to achieve whatever he could with whatever resources he had. He had moved from a self-defeating into a productive mode.

Another patient, Ms. R, illustrates this point of finding it less painful not to believe in a delusion. Ms. R had been dismissed from a company as she tried to advance within management. She went to live with her mother and was unsuccessful at finding another job that met her standards. She began to feel that she was "no good" and to experience some very alarming sensations. She believed that she had had a heart attack but could not find a doctor who agreed with her, and she was beginning to panic. In order to account for her sensations, she decided that some people with supernatural powers were trying to murder her. This, of course, was even more alarming, and she was angry and increasingly desperate when no one believed her. When we discussed this, I tried to get her back to the point where she had these sensations and to open her mind to explanations other than that of being the victim of a supernatural murder plot. I moved into a didactic mode and talked about how upsetting it could be to have to come home and start all over again. I stated that when people start to feel that they are "no good" for a period of time, it can be so stressful that they begin to experience a great deal of physical discomfort. I emphasized that people really underestimate the power of despair to create uncomfortable symptoms. I then asked if she wouldn't prefer to believe that her discomfort had been derived from her despair rather than believing that she had been the victim of a diabolical conspiracy. She said she would very much prefer to believe as I did rather than as she did but that she still believed in the plot. I asked her to help me persuade her of the less malignant explanation. One thing we agreed on was that, if she were still alive in three months, it would be less likely that anyone was trying to murder her. She agreed to try to think about it the way I suggested. She realized that she was so used to thinking about it the other way that it seemed natural to her. She could see that it set her apart from everybody, because she felt impelled to take legal action against her doctors for ignoring her condition but already knew that no lawyer would believe her. We talked about a future in which she had to resume this struggle versus a future in which she could set about trying to enjoy herself. She was somewhat attracted to the more enjoyable future.

Some people have the idea that reality is grim and that patients have it easier in life with their illness than they would without it. I think that hospital staff sometimes succumb to this idea when they are overworked and contemplating patients who seemingly have few responsibilities. I believe that, in order to be effective, a therapist has to understand that psychotic symptoms are very painful. Even though the patients' lives might seem free of responsibilities, they are often carrying a heavy emotional burden. A patient who regains her mental health has a lot of work to do to reestablish a normal life. In order to inspire her to do this, a therapist has to find a way to help the patient envision the enjoyments of moving a little closer to a mentally healthy ideal.

Did I argue with Mr. M and with Ms. R? Yes, in the sense of going over some arguments together. Did I argue with them directly about their delusions? Yes and no. If you spell out Mr. M's position fully, he was saying "I am hopelessly stupid and I got that way by being poisoned." I certainly did not take the position, "Yes, you are hopelessly stupid but you are not being poisoned." I took the position that there was not really any such thing as being hopelessly stupid. Having taken this position, there was really no reason to argue about the poisoning. Similarly with Ms. R — I did not agree that she was dying, so I didn't exactly argue with her about the reason she was dying. There is a quotation from Einstein that applies here: "Everything should be made as simple as possible, but not simpler" (Eisel & Reddig, 1981). The structure of a patient's argument is usually intricate. If the therapist oversimplifies it and goes round and round about the yes or no of being poisoned (or plotted against) without involving the issue of whether the patient is in fact hopeless (or dying), then the therapist is wasting time.

4

Hallucinations

This chapter details how I used a visual illusion to educate a patient about hallucinations. It also discusses helping patients who try to figure out the reason for their hallucinations.

A middle-aged woman with an impish look in her eye was knocking loudly on my office door.

"Doctor, can I come in and ask you a question?"

"Okay, come on in," I said.

To my delight, Ms. E asked me an important question.

"Doctor, I hear a voice. Does that make me crazy?"

"Only if you automatically believe what it says."

She laughed with pleasure.

"Do you think that someone must be sending the voice to you?" I asked her. "Do you believe that because you hear it, it must be out there?"

"Oh yes, definitely. It yells at me. Someone is out there yelling at me."

"You mean, it sounds as if someone is out there yelling at you?"

"Oh no, someone is really out there. I hear a voice."

"Well, I understand that you hear it. But just because you hear it doesn't mean it's really out there, does it?"

"Yes it does. Bye." She got up and left, smiling.

There was something very playful about her. I remembered a souvenir that I had brought back from San Francisco and made a mental note to dig it out of my closet and bring it to show her.

The next time she stopped by, I was ready for her.

"Doctor, can I come in?"

"Oh hi. Sure, come on in."

My souvenir looked a little like a flying saucer. It had a bowl-shaped bottom and a rounded top with a large circular hole in it. It was black on the outside, and the inside — top and bottom — was entirely lined with a reflective mirror surface. Whatever small flat object — for example, a penny — was placed at the middle of the bottom, it appeared to be, instead, on the surface of the top. As many times as I have seen it, it is still a shock when I try to touch the object and find that it isn't there.

"I have something I'd like to show you. Remember what we were talking about last time? Remember I was saying that just because you hear something doesn't mean it's really there?"

"Yes, but the voice is there. I hear somebody yelling at me."

"Would it be O.K. with you if I try to show you that our eyes and ears aren't perfect, that sometimes they can be tricked . . . that sometimes we can hear or see something that's not really there?"

"Sure." She moved closer to my desk, looking interested.

"Take a look at this," I said, moving my souvenir closer to her, "but don't touch it until I tell you to, O.K.?"

"O.K.," she said, looking at the image of the penny.

"O.K. Now, do you see the penny there on top?"

"Uh huh."

"Well, what would you say if I tried to tell you that the penny isn't real, that it's not really there?"

"I would say you were wrong."

"Well, would you like to go ahead and see if it's there? Go ahead. Try to touch it."

She tried, and, of course, she felt nothing and looked startled. She laughed delightedly.

"What do you call that?" she asked.

"A visual illusion."

"That's really neat. Well, I have to go. Bye."

"Bye."

Several weeks later I saw her sitting on her ward. She grinned and said hello.

"I still remember that illusion that you showed me. I really liked that. I like that word, 'illusion.' I was talking to the people in occupational therapy about it."

"Do you think that the voice could be an illusion?" I asked.

"What do you think?"

"Well, here at the hospital, we think of voices like the one you hear as being a symptom. What we mean is that they are like an illusion. We know that it sounds to you as if there is somebody yelling at you, but we believe that there really isn't anybody there."

"It sure sounds as if they're really out there."

"Well, didn't it look as if the penny was really there?"

"Yes, it sure did."

"Wouldn't it be nice to think that there wasn't really anybody out there yelling at you? Wouldn't it be less frightening to be mistaken about the voice than to be afraid of whoever might be yelling at you?"

"It would."

The next time I saw her, she smiled playfully as usual and said I had convinced her that the voice was an illusion. She continued to ask me questions on other topics but never mentioned the voice again.

Three years later, I saw her again. I was conducting a project and visited a local residential care facility. I saw a woman who looked slightly familiar but I did not realize who she was.

"Aren't you the lady who showed me that illusion at the hospital? I liked that."

Using our professional vocabulary, it is hard to assess what occurred. Was this therapy? I had not been involved with this patient in any kind of comprehensive way. She had not been on my ward. I was not present at her case conference, nor was there any record of our conversation in her chart. I had not known the circumstances of her admission. Nor had I known what diagnosis she had been given or what plans had been made for her discharge. Yet I had given her something to think about on a very important point, one that troubled her a great deal.

It might be argued that Ms. E was halfway to remission when I spoke with her, and that, although in a state of semi-remission she was capable of appreciating the information that I gave her, this information would not help her in the face of a recurrence of psychosis.

There is some basis for disagreement with this pessimistic conclusion. Research on state-dependent learning indicates that memory of a certain item is best when the person trying to remember it is in a state similar to when they learned it (Reus, Weingartner, & Post, 1979). When an individual undergoes a psychotic episode, she enters it by stages and then recovers by stages. Although the memory of our conversation might not be accessible to the patient when she is at her worst stage (if she undergoes future episodes), it might be accessible to her when she is in the sort of in-between stage that she was in when we talked. If, in the future, she were in such an in-between stage, but on her way into instead of out of a psychotic episode, her memory of our conversation might help her to realize that she was becoming ill.

The kind of education about illusions that I provided for this patient, helping her to question the compelling evidence of her own senses, is important for any hallucinating person to have. Unfortunately, it is not really a standard part of everybody's education, and it is not an easy concept to apply. Scientists learn to accept only information that has been objectively determined, but it is certainly true that this takes a lot of self-discipline and mutual communication. A scientist has good motivation to control his tendency to believe whatever seems true because he wants to continue in his profession. People who do not have this special motivation often do not do as well in restraining their belief in things that seem true but later turn out to be false. Hallucinating patients, like scientists, have a special reason to be exceptionally well-motivated to question things that only seem to be true. Hallucinating patients have much to gain from questioning their experiences because their experiences are frightening, and they would like to be reassured.

I am not stating that all hallucinating patients are receptive to discussion; this is certainly not the case. However, there are many patients who could benefit from this kind of discussion. If we have an attitude of pessimism about discussing hallucinations, these patients will remain undiscovered.

I am prepared to believe that the experience of hearing a voice is a very compelling one, and that, because the voice seems so real, there is a tendency to believe that it is coming from some outside source and to believe the contents of what it says. However, I do not think that we can properly conclude that patients can or cannot be educated in a way that makes these beliefs less compelling. The educability of each patient needs to be studied separately by trying to educate him and observing the results. We can experiment with convenient ways to do this, such as engaging a large group in a discussion and selecting only those who seem interested for further discussion. The implication of our current multifactor model of schizophrenia is that there are subsets of schizophrenic patients who can be reached in different ways. To take this model seriously would mean exposing large numbers of patients to different modes of treatment and selecting the ones who seem amenable for further efforts.

We can speculate that young people who are predisposed to schizophrenia might be helped if they could receive education about hallucinations before they actually experience them. There are many aspects of the experience of being human, even for those with no special genetic vulnerabilities, that are alarming to the individual who is not prepared for them. For example, young girls who are not forewarned about menstruation are likely to be terrified. With adequate preparation, the same experience will be accepted as normal. For someone who is genetically prone to hearing voices, this experience is, in a sense, normal for them. They are given no preparation for this because it is statistically rare in our society.

Sometimes I say to patients with a diagnosis of schizophrenia, "One in a hundred people hears voices." It startles them when I say this in a matter of fact way. I explain that some people's skin breaks out when they are upset, some people get ulcers, some get headaches, and some hear voices. This statement does not minimize the patient's suffering, but it places the suffering in the context of behavioral medicine rather than in the context of the supernatural.

Many patients who experience hallucinations become preoccupied with the question of why they are experiencing them. For example, Clifford Beers, in his book, *A Mind that Found Itself: An Autobiography*, tells of "phantasmagoric visions" that he saw at night during his mental illness (Beers, 1953, p. 30). He knew that the visions weren't real and sought an explanation for them. He concluded that they were produced by a "magic lantern" controlled by his "persecutors." Although he knew something was wrong with his mind, he nevertheless did not realize that these visions were symptoms of his illness. When a patient talks about his search for an explanation for his hallucinations, I question the patient about how he feels about his other characteristics, such as being tall or having blue eyes or freckles. I ask if he feels he must understand why he has freckles or blue eyes, and, usually, he says no. It can be soothing to realize that individual variations are not fully understood.

The person with an inquiring mind takes a lot of training before he will be satisfied with the kind of descriptive information that observation and science can provide, rather than always asking why. In the history of science, many authors whose intention was to discover the truth have fallen into the trap of trying to explain occurrences as unusual that are later found to be usual. The person who hears voices and thinks he has figured out that they are coming from the devil or the Russians or have been arranged by a meddling relative is making the same error as many pseudoscientists who have filled our libraries and bookstores with their volumes. The patient is assuming that something unexpected should not have occurred and would not have occurred without some special circumstance bringing it about, and he is assuming that he will be able to discover the nature of this special circumstance on his own.

Patients sometimes react to my statement that one in a hundred people hears voices by sitting back and taking a deep breath. It is easier to endure something if they feel it is just part of the hand they were dealt than if they feel that it was due to the malevolence of someone in their lives or to some critical error that they made.

Ms. E, whom I discussed earlier, was not an introspective person. She assumed the voices were real and she was angry at them for hollering at her. She had never thought of questioning her assumptions. Patients with a tendency toward analyzing their experiences, however, do not necessarily fare any better emotionally. I once treated a highly intelligent patient, Mr. A, who had tried intensively over the two years since he had had a psychotic episode to figure out why this had happened to him. It was interesting to compare the course of his speculations to the published literature on schizophrenia. He had essentially developed his own versions of an environmental hypothesis and a genetic hypothesis and was struggling to make them fit his own situation. He had not made much progress in putting his life back together. He seemed to feel that it was highly important for him to arrive at some conclusions in his speculations before he could safely go on with his life.

I emphasized in our discussion that he was trying to answer questions that even scientists with their research teams, equipment, and government grants had, thus far, been unable to resolve. I shared with him an article by Joseph Zubin, entitled "Chronic Schizophrenia from the Standpoint of Vulnerability," (1980) that was very helpful in refocusing his attention. Zubin's article emphasizes the intermittent nature of a psychotic condition in a particular individual. This defuses the search for etiology because the patient no longer must ask, "Why was I born a schizophrenic?" or "Did somebody's mistreatment stress me so badly that I turned into a schizophrenic?" Instead, he can ask, "What stress have I been exposed to recently that may have precipitated *this* episode?" without the implication that his life is ruined.

With educated patients or those who like to discuss things in detail, it is helpful to point out that no one understands the sequence of events in the brain that leads to hearing voices. The question of why a particular person is hearing a voice is essentially still a mystery. Knowing that this is still considered a mystery by those in authority may help the patient to stop trying to explain it with home-brewed explanations such as "my brother is talking to me over the television set."

When using the cognitive approach to therapy, the practitioner's knowledge of research can play a much more important role than simply endorsing the general cognitive approach. The client, with whatever degree of intellect he or she possesses, is forming a model of mankind in general, of himself or herself, and of psychopathology. Any of the latest scientific findings that the therapist can share in easily understandable language will help the patient to develop a model that is more successful in predicting his own behavior, well-being, and the behavior of others. (See Kingdon & Turkington, 1994, for some summaries of scientific findings about schizophrenia and ways of explaining these findings to patients.) The patients can tell when the therapist is taking their questions seriously. If we behave like pseudoscientists — that is, if we authoritatively pass on our latest rumors and cover up our uncertainties — we do not earn the patients' respect.

The experience of hearing voices may be very compelling to the patient, but why should it be so compelling to us? Why do many therapists get easily discouraged when they hear that the patient is psychotic? Certainly they do not do this on the basis of outcome studies; discussing patients' ideas about their voices has not been a focus of research. Is it truly scientific to assume that cognitive therapy, proven to alleviate the distress of depressed and anxious persons, will not be useful for the distress of psychotic persons? I believe that therapists are turning away from these patients, not because of research or clinical experience but because of hearsay.

This is an area where skepticism is needed. When we hear we can't talk to people about their hallucinations, we can ask what the scientific evidence is for that.

I have found that if I am not lulled into passivity by the unquestioning attitude of the patient, there are some simple suggestions that help the patient to take a step away from his or her hallucinations. When a patient says that the voices are saying something, if I say, "you mean it sounds as if there are voices saying something" this seems to slow down the patient in drawing psychotic conclusions. If the patient will cooperate with me, I ask him to say, "it sounds as if a voice is saying" every time they say, "a voice is saying." After a few sessions of this, the patient is able to get into the habit of speaking more precisely, and it seems to make the experience of hearing voices seem somewhat less compelling.

I don't believe that patients mind these interventions. The patient is well aware, mostly on the basis of nonverbal information such as skeptical glances, that she has not convinced others of the truth of her subjective experience. I believe that she experiences it as respectful when someone gives her the opportunity to discuss the status of her voices explicitly.

My interaction with Ms. E was comparatively easy because she specifically asked me about her voices, and her relationship with her voices
was unambiguously negative.

Some chronic patients have feelings about their voices that are more
mixed. A patient whose voices are a reminder of some romantic involvement, for example, may not feel ready to perceive voices as being unreal
and will not be able to do so without the kind of emotional support that
would be necessary to help someone in his efforts to end a nonreciprocal
relationship.

An interesting syndrome occurs when a patient begins to perceive his
voices as an object of worship. You can see in such patients a constant
process of theological disputation.

"My voices said the occupational therapist wouldn't be here today, but
she is, and my voices are always right. Maybe I heard it wrong."

This is a good opportunity to talk to the patient about how hard everybody tries to predict the future and how we have to accept uncertainties.

One man told me, "I could tell that the voice was really God because it
sounded so humble . . . after creating the whole universe and all the stars
and everything."

Because he seemed quite receptive to talking about it, I replied,
"Perhaps it was so humble because it really isn't God and didn't create
anything."

He chuckled appreciatively.

He told me about some kind of a test he constructed to prove that his
voice was God, something relating to what snacks his visitors would or
wouldn't bring the next day.

"You know," I told him, "for many years people have been trying to
make up tests to see whether God exists. Religious people say that God
has his own reasons for hiding. If there is a God, do you think that your
test is so clever that you can find him after all these other people
couldn't? Also, religious people feel that God wouldn't like these kinds
of tests."

The patient looked amused and nodded knowingly. These are interactions that you will not forget, and neither will the patient.

Oddly enough, when we talk about increasing patients' conversational
skills, we often mean teaching them how to make small talk. However,
sometimes the patients are immersed in thinking about critical cosmic or
spiritual questions that they believe to be more important than the ordinary matters that are the subject of most conversations. Patients are often
keenly interested in talking about these points. By discussing these
points with them, you are not introducing troublesome issues to people

who are otherwise content; in fact, these issues may be keeping them in a state of turmoil. For example, the patient who has the hypothesis that his hallucination is the voice of God has to struggle continually with his own incredulity because this hypothesis fits the behavior of his voices so badly. If you join him in this discussion, you are, at the very least, giving him some badly needed companionship, and possibly much more.

What the patient needs in order to set these ruminations to rest is some kind of an answer that satisfies him. It can be "God doesn't like to be tested," "I'm not the one to prove this," or "I'll just accept the doctor's word that the voices are a symptom" — whatever helps the patient to clear his mind. When the patient's mind has been cleared, it is then much easier for him to begin to pay attention to the kinds of constructive practical activities that will give him a growing basis for small talk and ordinary everyday social behavior.

5

Some Deviant Belief Systems

This chapter relates the cases of a man who believed that clumsy people should stay out of everybody's way and a man who got into trouble for mocking ordinary attitudes. It discusses developing custom-tailored responses for unusual beliefs.

A Chinese psychiatrist that I once worked with told me about a Chinese tradition that fascinated me. He said that a man at the height of his professional competence might consider retiring into private life at that point, before he begins to offer less than his best performance. It seems to me that in psychiatric circles, at least, we do not have a similar concept of a type of withdrawal that is not antisocial but that is based upon a high order of social feeling. I am not sure if such a man would receive the honor he expected if he retired in a milieu where risk-taking was more highly valued. In such a milieu, he might be considered perfectionistic; people might ask "what has he done lately?"

The idea of a deliberate withdrawal has a certain romance when it is done voluntarily by someone in a milieu where it is understood and honored. It is sad when it takes place because an individual misunderstands his milieu and thinks that it is expected or even forced. I once worked with a patient, Mr. S, who had an ideology of withdrawal. He believed that because he was clumsy he was supposed to stay out of other people's way. He used to stay in his bedroom and read. He felt genuinely afraid of leaving his room because he believed that others shared his conviction that a clumsy person should stay out of the way, and he feared that they would be angry with him if he emerged. He also felt that because he didn't work he was not entitled to food. He continually tried to eat less. He seemed surprised to hear that people value trying, whether success is reached or not. He was also surprised that some people would be angry with him for not trying, rather than appreciating his consideration for locking himself away. It seemed to make him less frightened when he heard that his ideology was not typical.

In a session of rational emotive behavior therapy (REBT) with a typical patient, the therapist would call the patient's attention to his use of "should" and "supposed to" to help alleviate some of the patient's unnecessary misery. In the case of Mr. S, the removal of the "should" statements may have made him feel a little less pressured. Instead of thinking, "I should stay in my room," he would think, "it is better to stay in my room because I don't want anybody angry at me." Presumably, he could then feel a little less miserable because he could feel he was cleverly making the most of his experience under the circumstances, instead of feeling it was his fate. However, deleting the "should" and "supposed to" would not be sufficient to restore Mr. S to a full life.

It is not just that Mr. S had a lot of "should" statements in his mind. There were two additional problems: his "should" statements were very atypical, and he didn't know just how atypical they were.

Of course, it is part of traditional REBT to share with the patient what a crazy world it is. When the patient has not been able to figure this out for himself, the therapist can really help if he or she gives the patient the details, not just about his own irrationalities but also about the irrationalities of others. To a patient like this, I might say, "Most people have this funny thing about working. They believe that everyone should do his part every day, and they are angry when someone doesn't try. If you don't eat, they get even angrier, because if you weaken yourself you can't get out and try to work every day. Even if when you try to work you make such a mess of things that it takes five people to clean up after you, they still think that a good person is one who gets out and tries to work every day. They don't think of it the way you do, that you are saving them work by not working and that because you aren't going to work, you shouldn't eat."

This can be very amusing to the patient. Each value system has its merits and its absurdities. If the patient can understand the absurdities of the majority belief system, and especially the absurdities of the interface between the majority belief system and his own, this will help him to get along. Mr. S, if he understood this well, would no longer expect to be honored for hiding in his room. He would feel more entitled to venture out and make some mistakes. He might still believe that it would be a better world if everyone followed his system, but he would at least know that this is not the case.

I once worked with an extremely lucid young man, Mr. C, who had a diagnosis of schizophrenia and who was rather cheerful. He said that he heard voices but that they were very nice, divine voices that took his part and made him feel good. He had no money and no relatives who could help. The staff seemed to believe that he couldn't take care of himself. There was some hint that he might be a firesetter, but he seemed rather capable in some ways. He was the only patient that I worked with at that particular hospital who went out on pass and worked at a part-time job during the day. I questioned him about the details of this firesetting episode. Apparently his mother had come to his apartment and found a burnt area on the carpet. I had assumed from what I had heard that it was a large area and that she was afraid that his misuse of alcohol or drugs had led him to fall asleep while smoking. He stated that the burn on the carpet was very small. He also emphasized that he had put out the fire himself; he had not had to be rescued by his mother, nor had she found it smoldering.

I did not see the carpet. The circumstances of the fire's starting, the size of the burn, and how the fire was stopped remain a mystery. Further inquiry revealed something about the patient's attitude that his mother may have found alarming.

I asked him how he reacted when his mother found the burn in the carpet.

The patient snickered and said, "I said, 'so what, who cares?' I couldn't understand why she was so upset. I wasn't hurt. It was just a carpet. It was just a cigarette burn."

Sometimes patients get in trouble not just for having irrational thoughts that most people don't have but also for not having the commonplace irrationalities that are almost universal. When someone does not share one of these, the other person is startled and alarmed. There is a joke that goes, "What time is it when the clock strikes thirteen? Time to get a new clock!" Unexpected beliefs are jarring to the bystander. Something about the patient is different, and who knows how far their differences might go? Ordinarily, we do not have to examine every belief that someone has in order to judge whether we can depend on them. If they agree with us on a few major things, we assume that they believe many of the standard things that most of us agree on. Even disagreements are standardized. We recognize certain commonplace beliefs that we might not share. But if someone veers off sharply from what we expect, even on something that is not that important, their status becomes questionable; after this, the unpredictable person is not considered dependable until his competencies have been explored in detail. Because no one actually knows how to do this, or takes the time to do so, it is possible that their status remains questionable indefinitely.

Mr. C was in need of REBT for his own irrationalities, but, in order to avoid being stigmatized by others, he also needed some candid explanations of their irrationalities as well. I told him that damage to a major household object is taken as a near-catastrophe by many people. It is customary in some circles to get very upset about any event that could have led to bodily danger, even if it didn't. After hearing the way in which he talked to his mother that day, I could see how she could have become alarmed. By laughing it off, he made it sound as if he would take no precautions in the future. In general, he had a kind of jeering manner toward the foibles of others; we had talked about his manner before. He used to go around staring at the nurses and laughing at them. We talked about how, just as people in quaint little towns don't like tourists who just gape at them and seem to find them funny, the nurses were also uncomfortable with his attitude toward them. If he could only anticipate the irrationalities of his mother and others, instead of being so openly amused and astonished, he could fare much better.

Sometimes a patient's unusual belief can cause a problem between patient and therapist, even if it is a rational belief. Some patients will say, rather bitterly, "I don't need anybody." I have had a few patients who said this and then looked at me, expecting an argument. A therapist might be expected to try to find out more about the negative emotions behind such a statement and to convince the patient that relationships are very important. However, if the patient really feels alone in his life, he or she is not prepared to hear about the importance of something that currently seems unattainable. You can start off very well with such a patient and immediately let him know that you are different from what he expected by agreeing with his provocative statement. "Yes, you are absolutely right. You don't need anybody." Hesitate for a bit to let it sink in that you are not going to argue before making the point that may start a discussion. "You certainly don't need anybody in your life, and it's good to keep that in mind, but you do want some people to care about you, don't you?" It is much easier to engage the patient in a discussion about his relationships with other people on this realistic basis.

We can regard many strange psychotic behaviors — wearing weird clothes, living in the street, and so on — as reactions that almost seem designed to convince someone that the patient doesn't need the approval of others, that he doesn't need certain people to take care of him, and so on. Helping the patient to develop these convictions on a verbal level may alleviate his need to be a living demonstration of these points.

Many patients feel that, in the secular context of psychiatric thought, their religious beliefs are considered deviant. One patient, smiling slyly, asked me before a workshop if Jesus Christ would have been considered psychotic according to the diagnostic manual. Others, as if ready to forego interacting with me immediately if I give the wrong answer, immediately question me about my personal state of religious belief before talking to me. I think what they really want to know is whether, within the context of our dialogue, I will be accepting toward their beliefs. This is a critical issue for many patients. Although in the diagnostic manual for psychiatry (American Psychiatric Association, 1994) it states that religious beliefs particular to an individual's culture are not to be considered symptoms, many patients have observed that individual mental health workers may have negative feelings about such beliefs. Some patients are on the lookout for signs that a particular person will not accept their beliefs, and they will not confide in or be influenced by such people.

"Every time I would tell the psychiatrist how I felt, he'd say, 'there you go again with those religious beliefs,'" a woman told me. She looked amused that this man could have been a psychiatrist. She expected psychiatrists to be a lot more understanding.

The ability to listen and communicate within a religious frame of reference can expand the range of patients that a therapist can reach. The religious frame of reference is highly developed and usually has within it answers for problems that individuals thinking in this context will encounter.

For example, a young woman told me she was afraid to go outside by herself. When I inquired about what she was afraid of, she stated that she was afraid of being kidnapped and tortured. As we talked, she volunteered that she believed she would have these experiences because she is Christian, and many people have been martyred because of their Christianity. When I inquired about whether she believed that an innocent person who was martyred because of her Christianity could expect to go to heaven, she immediately brightened.

"Can we go over that again?" she asked.

We went over it a few times until she grasped the point. Her fear arose only when she was thinking partially in a religious context. If she totally accepted her religious frame of reference to the extent of expecting to be rewarded for her martyrdom, she no longer experienced an incapacitating apprehension.

In cognitive therapy, we develop custom-tailored responses in collaboration with the patient to soothe the unnecessarily painful emotions that have been stirred by the patient's irrational worries. Secular worries can be answered with secular responses. Sometimes religious worries need a religious response (see Propst, Ostrom, Watkins, Dean, & Mashburn, 1992).

Patients brought up within a religious frame of reference are one example of patients who are not automatically respectful of a psychiatric frame of reference. There are, of course, many others as well who do not recognize the authority of those who have them in custody.

I remember one woman with particular vividness. She had been a health professional in a hospital and had left under bitter circumstances. She had been ill afterward and had suffered greatly from postoperative complications that may not have been necessary. She was furious about having to be in a psychiatric hospital. When the psychiatrist was briefly testing her mental status, he asked her the date. She looked at him contemptuously, looked around the room to see if anyone else understood her, and replied correctly in German rather than in English, hoping to create a demonstration that she knew more than he did.

In individual sessions, this woman's thinking demonstrated a complete non-acceptance of the world the way it is currently organized and a "let's start all over again" approach toward fixing it.

With regard to the hospital, she suggested that it be completely reorganized. All of the personnel with kindly dispositions who got along well with patients, whether they were currently psychiatrists, housecleaners, or kitchen workers, would be placed in positions where they could work with patients. All the others, despite their current positions, would be in charge of taking care of the building, supplies, and so on.

A patient who harbors the bitter suspicion that almost everything is a big mistake has a large burden to bear, because she can trust only herself and must, therefore, do everything that needs to be done by herself. It eases her pain greatly if the therapist can appreciate that some of her grievances and ideas for improvement have a lot of merit. When she sees that a person who is more a part of organized society than she is can understand her and recognize her merits, she feels some relief and may be willing to resume communication with the normal society that she had written off as hopeless.

6

Anger

This chapter discusses helping chronic patients cope with their situation — no friends, no job, no transportation, no home, no money, no clothes, no furniture, and no respect.

The life situation of chronic patients is often deplorable. In addition to the suffering inherent in their symptoms, they often suffer from the accumulated problems of years of illness — no friends, no job, no transportation, no home, no money, no clothes, no furniture, and, as the comedian Rodney Dangerfield says, "no respect." Often their families have exhausted their financial and emotional resources and cannot do more for them.

This situation provides the greatest possible challenge to the therapist's belief in the cognitive method of therapy. Unless a therapist truly believes what Albert Ellis says — that only a few things such as food, shelter, and air are absolutely necessary to human existence — the therapist may find himself or herself at a loss to believe that the patients can feel any happier in their situation. Many of the sad stories told by the chronically mentally ill have to do with the some of the extraordinary hurts that they have endured at the hands of others. It is very easy, in listening to these stories, to become angry along with the patients instead of helping them be less angry. However, if the therapist holds fast to a cognitive view of the patients' emotions and helps the patients to be less angry, there will be noticeable improvements. The patients' situation may still be the same in terms of having no place to go, no possessions, and so on, but suddenly they are smiling, working on arts and crafts projects, getting along with the nurses, and going on trips to the museum. The therapist is left wondering, "what was wrong with me that I thought this was so hopeless?"

Ms. D's record indicated that, during her admissions to the hospital, she had been in restraints for long periods of time because of explosive temper outbursts. Yet, when she wasn't angry, she was very playful. There was a twinkle in her eye, and she enjoyed just kidding around. She also had a lot of strength of character; despite some annoying chronic medical problems and handicaps that she patiently endured, she was always working on self-improvement projects. She would write down new words, study them, and practice them.

Often, when someone is angry, she loses the ability to think of her actions in terms of costs and benefits. For example, Ms. D became furious one day because of a telephone call. She found out on the telephone about a financial loss of several hundred dollars. She became so incensed that she ended up in restraints, and any thoughts that the staff may have had about allowing her to be discharged in the near future were set aside indefinitely. To her, the amount lost seemed like an astronomical sum, and so, even as she lay in restraints the next day, it still seemed reasonable to her to have exploded. She had not compared the amount to anything in particular; it just seemed like an enormous loss.

I said to her that the money was "chickenshit" compared to her freedom. She seemed quite surprised that I said this. It made her laugh a lot, not just because of the language I used, but, I believe, because the concept I was introducing was liberating. She saw that she had something of great value that she hadn't counted before, her reputation, and that by blowing up, she had given that away (though only temporarily). Instead of feeling several hundred dollars poorer, she now felt inestimably richer.

We went over this reasoning repeatedly during the next few weeks, and I believe that Ms. D derived a great deal of benefit from this. When things bothered her, she would always say "that's chickenshit" and start laughing.

I had a chance to talk to Ms. D after she had been out of the hospital for several weeks. She reported that some of her relatives who had been taking care of her children for her now trusted her more and she was getting to see the children more often. She seemed extremely pleased with herself.

The chronic patient who cannot control her anger falls into a situation where she essentially loses all of her rights. She is so angry about everything that her complaints can hardly be taken seriously. Because she is so angry at everyone, she elicits anger in others. The fact that she elicited this does not make it hurt any less. When she tells her stories of how others were angry at her, these stories sound very improbable to people who have not observed this kind of vicious cycle occur, so that at times she is not believed, and this makes her even angrier.

When the patient tells stories about how she has been treated, it is important for the therapist to realize that even the most improbable details may be true, but some information may be missing. The patient may reveal this later when she is feeling better. For example, a patient once told me that her father chained her to her bed and wouldn't let her take her medication. When she was feeling better, she filled in the missing detail that she had threatened to commit suicide by taking an overdose of her medication. Similarly, a young woman once told me that it upset her that her boyfriend stayed out all night. Later, she told me that she had threatened him, "Some night I am going to kill you while you are asleep."

If you keep your mind open to the patients' stories, you will gain more and more experience at piecing them together. One patient, who had a terrible reputation in his home town for being a violent, dangerous character, was committed to the hospital. He kept repeating over and over, "I wasn't doing anything. I was just walking down the street carrying two containers of milk when the police picked me up." After I had gained more experience with the process of commitment, I could understand such stories better. Often, someone may complain about the patient, but it may take several days to get the necessary documentation before having the police go get the patient. By then the patient may be engaged in some utterly innocuous activity, so that he cannot understand why he is being taken to the hospital.

When patients cannot comprehend why something is happening to them, they may have a tendency to fill in the gap with delusional elaboration. I remember a patient that our team interviewed almost immediately after he had arrived at the hospital. He told a characteristic story of desperation and confusion, in which he left out the details of his own behavior but could only remember the behavior of others, which puzzled him extremely. He had an argument with family members, left the house, and wandered about for some time. He went into a local hospital to use the bathroom and had somehow called attention to himself in such a way that the police were called. Somehow this led to the police chasing him into a local park. Somewhere along the chase, he began to believe that the policemen were "not human, possibly from outer space," and he reacted by throwing things at them. He explained that, because he didn't feel that their action in chasing him was justified, and because he believed that policemen would only behave in a justifiable manner, he concluded that they were "not real" policemen and, therefore, "not human." His elaboration is an imaginative way of saying "this shouldn't be happening," that gets expanded to "this couldn't be happening," and leads to "it only seems as if this is happening; really something else is happening."

Many mental health workers, without realizing it, take the part of the other people in the patient's story. Because the story sounds unbelievable, they think that the patient may be fabricating. The patient can easily tell that his story is not believed by the fact that a mental health worker glosses over it instead of trying harder to understand it.

Possibly, therapists are afraid that, if they show interest in the patient's story, they will influence the patient in the direction of unreality. They simply pay little attention to the story, hoping that, as the patient improves through medication, his account of how he got into the hospital will be somehow changed. Often, however, even though the patient's reasoning ability improves over the course of his hospital stay, he is not thoughtful enough to rethink the conclusions he formed during his psychotic episode. Unless someone helps him to do this, the conclusions drawn during his psychosis may remain a part of his thinking indefinitely.

In trying to help the patient to understand the series of events that led to his hospitalization, it often turns out that the patient has a very low awareness of the ordinary human frailties of other people. By explaining the other person's behavior to the patient on the basis of the other person's ordinary limitations, the therapist gives the patient less reason to be angry at others because their behavior no longer has to be explained by postulating extraordinary malevolence. At the same time, the patient feels that the therapist understands his point of view and is not on the other person's side.

The patient's perfectionistic ideas about how people behave can leave her genuinely baffled in a crisis. The young woman whose father tied her to the bed was apparently unaware of her ability to induce a state of complete desperation in her father. The patient carrying the milk containers had no idea of how he had frightened people by swinging a bat or of how long it took before they could do anything about it.

Many of the stories that chronic patients tell concern events that occurred on the ward. Thus, the therapist is in the potentially awkward position of listening to a story about another staff member. However, this situation can be turned to therapeutic advantage. One patient that I treated in an inpatient setting believed that the nurses were calling her obscene names. The patient and I would go to the ward and talk to the nurses together. When we openly asked the nurses if they had said these very unlikely things, they denied it and seemed friendly, and the patient seemed reassured. The patient was often in the position of having to make repeated demands upon the staff, and her impatience often created a helpless, irritable feeling on the part of the staff. She may indeed have received some exasperated glances, but she had perceived the staff's feelings as being more overtly hostile and more long-lasting than they really were. Just the experience of seeing the nurse when the nurse was no longer directly under pressure and was receptive was valuable to the patient. She became less angry because she realized that she had exaggerated the event she was angry about. We had to repeat this many times, and it seemed to temporarily restore her very fragile relationships with the ward staff. This intervention was not, for this patient, a permanent improvement, but it served as a means of maintaining reasonable wellbeing.

Often the events that the patient reports have occurred on the ward exactly as they say and will very likely continue to occur. Many patients have the idea that, because they are in a hospital, the staff should behave in a manner that makes their circumstances ideal from an emotional point of view. Patients who have never before been hospitalized at a public institution are surprised to find themselves in a situation where they cannot get attention when they want it, it is noisy, they are in danger of being robbed or assaulted, and they are badgered by other patients for money and cigarettes. It is certainly worth taking the time to explain to such a patient, just as you would to a new intern (who is also likely to be astonished) some of the factors that lead to it being hard to change the situation. It is also worth explaining that the staff understands that the situation is far from ideal.

However, some chronic patients with years of experience in public institutions still react with amazement at the things that typically occur there. Oddly enough, they actually feel better if you explain to them just how low their status really is. Because they haven't grasped this, they are continually taken off guard, thinking that they should be treated as equals. I find that reading the work of sociological observers of the hospital scene, for example, *Being Mentally Ill* by Thomas Scheff (1966), alerts me to phenomena concerning the interaction between people of different status that I can then share with my patients. I can say to the patient, "you are the patient, so everything you do counts against you. Yes, you are right. If a staff member gets angry, it doesn't count, but if you get angry, it counts against you." This must be said sympathetically. The two of you must share the idea that if you could design things, you would make it different, but that the way things are, certain rules apply. When a patient reports that a staff member was grouchy, you can discuss how nice it would be if staff members were never grouchy but that thinking "it should be that way" is only going to make the patient feel more frustrated.

I have found that imagery seems especially helpful in anger management. At times, when I provide a patient with an image that conveys his helplessness with respect to the staff, instead of showing a negative emotion, he seems to be amused. For example, I once treated a young man who was in the hospital because he had manifested a violent temper in an argument with his girlfriend. He had a discussion with the psychiatrist that turned into an argument. The patient insisted upon something that the psychiatrist disagreed with, and the psychiatrist thought that the patient was uncooperative and unready to leave. The patient was angrily telling me how he was right and the psychiatrist was wrong. I asked him to imagine that he was in the same position as Fay Wray in the classic version of the movie King Kong, that is, that he was in the palm of a giant. I asked if he would tickle King Kong. Would he scratch him, if he was in his hand? He said that he certainly wouldn't. Somehow I conveyed to him that his situation was more like being in the hand of King Kong than being two equals.

The next day he had another conversation with the psychiatrist, and it went very amiably. He stopped at my office to tell me about it, and he seemed very happy. He did not seem at all like someone who had learned a bitter truth — that he had to be obsequious. Instead, he seemed like someone who had gained mastery of something that he had never understood. He had achieved something, and he looked very proud. Many patients lack an intuitive understanding of power differences. Explaining to him what may have seemed obvious to many others helped him to find his way around obstacles that were previously invisible to him.

Patients who misinterpret assertiveness as always winning are constantly disappointed and humiliated. One of the most valuable preparations for assertiveness is being able to evaluate the amount of leverage that you can exert in a situation. If you have none, you are not in a position to make demands.

Some people think that rational emotive behavior therapy (REBT) and assertiveness are opposite ways of dealing with a similar situation. They think that assertiveness helps you to get what you want and REBT is a way of consoling yourself for not getting what you want rather than going after it. This is not correct.

Paradoxically, for the patient in a very low status, REBT increases his leverage in a bargaining situation. I once saw a patient on a locked ward win an argument with a psychiatrist. The psychiatrist was saying to the patient that if he did some particular thing, he could have a pass off the ward for an hour. The patient said, "I don't care. Leave me on the locked ward." The psychiatrist, of course, had no answer for this. Because the reinforcer had been rejected, the therapist was now the one who had no leverage.

If a patient approaches the psychiatrist asking to leave the hospital with the attitude, "I have to get out of here; I can't stand it another minute," the patient cannot bargain at all because he cannot compromise. However, if he convinces himself that he doesn't have to get off the ward but only wants to, then he can negotiate with the psychiatrist. He may say, for example, "If you give me privileges today and I do well, how about a discharge in a few days?"

When an angry patient feels desperate about something he wants from the staff, I am often reminded of an old movie. A man is imprisoned on an island. His sentence is fairly short — perhaps a month. However, he gets to thinking about his girlfriend and how beautiful she is until he feels he can't stand it in prison any more, so he breaks out of the prison and swims back to the mainland for a short time with her. He is apprehended and brought back to the island, and his sentence is increased to about six months. Once again, he feels he cannot be away from her, breaks out, and is apprehended again. This takes place over and over, and each time his sentence is lengthened until it is practically a life sentence.

Why is it that the demanding quality of desperate patients makes it so hard for them to get what they want? How exactly do the irrational thoughts "I must have this" or "I can't stand it if I don't" result in actually reducing the person's chances of getting what they want? Possibly this is because when someone feels this way, the other person feels as if she is being told, "You must give this to me." Instead of giving in because the other wants it so badly, the person reacts to the irrational statements of need by pulling the opposite way, as if to demonstrate that the patient doesn't need it, but only wants it. After all, if we were to grant things according to how badly people wanted them, the more rational people would be constantly at the mercy of the less rational. There seems to be an instinctive reaction to refuse such requests in order to avoid a phenomenon known as psychotic tyranny, where a psychotic person completely dominates those around him by the strength of his irrational desires.

Although it is often possible in a particular instance to quiet things down by granting the patient something that he is demanding, it is inevitable that a patient who comes across in this manner will repeatedly trigger the very common reaction of refusal. It is rare, in the middle of an argument with a patient, for the other person to be able to say to the patient, "You don't need this, you only want this, but I will give it to you anyway because I would like to." It is much more common for the ordinary person to react as leaders do to terrorist demands — refuse.

It is easy for a patient who has fallen into a habit of feeling urgent about his wants to develop the idea that everybody hates him. Observing the patient interacting with the ward staff, the therapist might be able to see how the patient came to such a conclusion. However, when the patient changes his belief that he "must" have what he wants or that he "can't stand" not getting what he wants, his demeanor undergoes a change. He becomes polite, and the situation changes rapidly. Ward staff change their responses almost immediately.

Explaining to patients why they are getting negative reactions consists of describing the limits of normal patience. "People just hate to be told what to do. The nurse is just a person. When you told her what to do she told you she didn't have to. I'll bet if you asked her instead of telling her, and you really meant it, she might act differently. Do you think she should be like an angel and not notice when you tell her what to do? I think that would be nice but I haven't found a way to make that happen," or "Yes, the nurse was probably not friendly to you today. It was only this morning that you yelled at her. Maybe if you talk to her nicely for a few days in a row, she'll begin to trust you again. Yes, it would be nice if she could do that right away, but usually it takes a while. That's just the way people are. Yes, wouldn't it be nice if they could forget faster? Wouldn't it be nice if someone could forget faster just because she is a nurse?"

In a way, these statements are a confrontation because the patient's poor management of the situation is highlighted. However, the patient perceives the therapist as being on his side because the limitations of the nurse are acknowledged. At first, I used to feel self-conscious about discussions such as this because I felt I might be letting the nurse down by discussing her with the patient. However, after several experiences where I met with a nurse and a patient together, I saw that the nurse felt supported by my statements. I was giving her permission to act human and to be accepted as such, and this was welcome.

Many therapists feel reluctant to work on anger management with chronic patients because they feel that it is an unacceptable compromise. They feel that the circumstances of the chronic patient's life must be improved and that helping them adjust to these deplorable conditions is not only hopeless but also morally questionable. I have been vulnerable to these arguments at times, and at those times I was not as effective with my patients. Once, in listening to the grievances of a woman who had been asked to leave a boarding home, I was distracted from her altogether by a fantasy of operating my own boarding home, where, of course, everyone would be understood. To be an effective psychotherapist, you have to be willing to help the patient compromise with the circumstances of her life. This is, after all, what we mean by accepting reality.

Being angry is a crippling, unpleasant experience. We do not know much about the biochemistry of contentment. However, there is a feeling, familiar to those who know how to manage fear and anger, of gladness to be alive, an interest in simple things, and a readiness to smile. This state of mind is disrupted by anger. It is bad enough that these patients have to endure their deplorable circumstances. Why should they also have to suffer the absence of contentment? A therapist who acquires experience in anger management knows that this state of contentment can be achieved even under bad circumstances. Far from keeping the patients from advancing their circumstances, it actually helps them to advance. For example, if a patient has been sociable and pleasant on the ward for a while and an opportunity to move out into the community becomes available, the patient is high on the social worker's list. If a patient is sociable and pleasant over a period of time, he may begin to have pleasant, friendly interactions with other patients that he would have completely missed if he had continued to come across as continually angry.

Many times in the course of my career I have run across patients who reminded me of Al Pacino in the movie "And Justice for All." In that movie, Pacino is defending a client whom he believes is innocent. As the movie goes on, he gets more and more information leading to the conclusion that his client is guilty and has been lying to him all along. He gets so angry that, on the day of the trial, the truth bursts out of him. As he is summing up his defense for the jury, he suddenly starts shouting "he's guilty." In the final scene, we see Pacino sitting on the steps of the courthouse and we understand that his career may be over. His moment of abandon may have cost him his role in the legal system.

There are many patients who pass through the hospital whose lives show a decline. At some past time, their lives were fuller. Possibly they were married with children and a career. Then, somehow, they were faced with a compromise that they were unable to make, and they lost some of what they had and, often, went into a tailspin and lost the rest as well. Sometimes they develop a bitterness, which, if you ask about their earlier life, you find was not always there.

After working in inpatient settings, I have come to realize that the hospital can serve as an in-between place where people end up when it doesn't work out for them anywhere else. There are many patients who are not psychotic but whose life structures outside have been ruined by some crucial event in adulthood from which they did not recover. Most of them have heard ordinary advice, but the advice hasn't worked for them because they are unusual people. The therapist has to be like an optometrist — she has to help the patient custom-design a stress management strategy that works for an unusual mentality. Like eyeglasses, this strategy may work only for this patient and not for anyone else.

If we regard life as balancing on a tightrope and the typical kinds of advice as being the net, those in the hospital have fallen through the net. At any given time, depending upon what kinds of people are thought to fit into society, different kinds of people will fall off the tightrope and through the net.

When I first started as an inpatient therapist, I treated several ex-whistleblowers. Possibly that was a time when cynicism was more rampant and idealists were having a hard time. Later on, I had a caseload of patients who had been involved in criminal activity. I have not run into many cases recently of crossed idealists, but I think that many patients perceive themselves in this way, and it is useful to know how to approach this type of case.

One man in his thirties had worked for a government organization and lost his job after reporting the misdeeds of some of his coworkers to higher authorities. When something goes wrong, it is natural to think that we must have been wrong. Unfortunately, in his case, this tendency may have been reinforced by others. He had the impression that well-meaning friends and an extremely long string of therapists (this patient stated that he had seen approximately 20 therapists) all felt that he should not have done what he did and should move in the direction of becoming an ordinary, loyal organization member. He felt they had tried to convince him that being idealistic was childish and masochistic, and a grown-up must do whatever he has to do to maintain his career. Instead of feeling relieved of his burden of being unusually idealistic, he more or less dropped out. He felt put down by the advice he had received; he was unable to think of a way of defending himself against the charges of being impractical, childish, and overly idealistic.

In order to move on with his life, he needed a new way of conceptualizing what he had done. He was having trouble because he felt that what he had done was right, and he didn't want to change himself in an unfavorable direction. At the same time, in order to have confidence in his future, he needed to feel that he had learned something. Because he was idealistic rather than materialistic, I thought that he might easily understand an analogy between his desire for justice and someone else's desire for a certain object. I asked him whether he would look down on somebody who wanted a diamond that he could not afford. He said it wasn't wrong to want it, and just because you couldn't have it didn't mean that you shouldn't have wanted it. Then we applied this to what he wanted. He could see that the desire for justice was like the desire for a diamond. There was nothing wrong with wanting it. Justice, like the diamond, was something very beautiful and, to the person who wanted it, worth a certain amount of striving, sacrificing, and waiting. However, like the diamond, sometimes the price was so high that someone might decide that the time was not ripe to acquire it. If someone lacked support from others and could see that the chance that his sacrifice would bring about justice was unlikely, he might decide to wait for better circumstances.

The patient liked this way of looking at the question. It enabled him to see his action as a good one but to regard the future without feeling that he would always have to suffer negative consequences. After all, why should he bother getting started in a new career if he was going to do the same thing and get fired again. At the same time, the analogy of an expensive luxury gave him hope that the future would not involve only compromises. From time to time, with careful planning, he might be able to afford some extravagant idealistic action.

This way of seeing the problem enabled the patient to improve. He had felt trapped by the anticipation of the actions that he might take in the future if he became angry again. He had become rather indifferent to his own future and had been content to drift from one therapist to another and, finally, into the hospital. When he felt free of the need to take the same actions again in the same circumstances, he became more animated and willing to leave the hospital and try again.

In his case, his disapproval of his coworkers' misdeeds had not led to temper outbursts but to actions. Behind his clinical presentation of a person in a state of stagnation, was the thought "these kinds of things must not occur." When he described what had happened to him he did not become overtly angry. The therapist does not have to wait until the angry thoughts are expressed more conventionally to teach the patient to manage them. If you can recognize angry thoughts in different guises, your patient will be spared the trouble of translating them into ordinary reactions. It is not serious that he reacts in a different manner. It is only serious that he has not learned to manage his reaction and that he lives in fear of his own behavior.

I treated another patient, Mr. P, who had also lost his long-standing job on a matter of principle. He came across in a more angry manner. After losing his job as a result of reporting some fraudulent practices and losing his wife to a professional person to whom they had turned for help, he had fallen upon hard times and was living in a trailer camp. He quarreled continually with his neighbors and was involved in several ongoing lawsuits. In the hospital, he became angry very easily. When he talked about the immediate past, he made the trailer camp sound like a jungle where battles were always occurring. I do not recall that he had any delusional beliefs, but he took offense at every possible thing. He had found his way into a milieu where there were other like-minded people, and it was easy to start a quarrel.

This was not just a matter of an unassertive person being taken advantage of and then trying to learn assertiveness. The sheer number of quarrels into which he was increasingly drawn indicated that arguments were no longer an interruption but had, instead, become a major life goal.

Using a cognitive or REBT approach, it is possible to work with patients without lengthy explorations of situations that no longer engage their day-to-day attention. In this patient's case, his prior interpersonal context — a longstanding job and marriage — had completely slipped away from him. These losses were the occasion for his drawing some bitter conclusions. It is these conclusions, not the losses, that are causing his current nightmarish adjustment.

In questioning this patient about his adjustment before his disillusionment, I had the impression that it was precisely because he had little experience with bitterness that he had so much difficulty dealing with it once it occurred. He had been easygoing before the events in question. It took an unusually traumatic set of events to make him bitter, and this made it difficult for him to recover from the bitterness, because the events were so bad that they seemed to justify the bitterness. I have encountered many patients who claim that before a certain event their lives were completely different, and often the family has corroborated this. Sometimes a young person who is gifted, for example, has almost no difficulty with anything and virtually no experience dealing with failure until a setback occurs in early adulthood, from which they seem to have little power to recover. I have pointed out to several such patients that they missed out on experience with failure. The other children who weren't as talented as they are learned much earlier in life how to pick themselves up after a fall. Failure is like a childhood disease. If you get it for the first time in adulthood, it seems a lot more serious, but after recovery, you are just as immune as someone who developed immunity in childhood.

I gave Mr. P an analogy to express my idea of how his disillusionment had affected his life. Suppose there were two adjoining countries, Country A and Country B. The customs of the two countries were entirely different. In Country A, everyone was very kind and considerate and this was expected. In Country B, it was every man for himself. In Country B, you couldn't expect anyone else to look out for your interests. The rules were that everybody tried as hard as he could to advance only his own interests, and it was up to you to keep the other person from taking advantage of you. Mr. P nodded and seemed interested.

The people of both of these countries understood the difference in customs between them. If someone from Country B crossed over into Country A they were shunned, because no one there wanted to have anything to do with someone who wasn't considerate of the other person's interests. If someone from Country A crossed over into Country B, whether they were hurt by the Country B citizens or not depended upon how they behaved. If they continued to act considerate as they did in their own country, their innocence was respected. The Country B citizens did not consider them fair game, and they courteously escorted them back to the border. If, however, the Country A citizen wandering in Country B tried to fend for himself and got in anybody's way, he usually got the worst of it. Unskilled in the competitive ways of Country B, he lost one confrontation after another.

Mr. P had somehow wandered into Country B when he became disillusioned. Instead of shunning aggressive people, the way he would have in Country A, he got competitively involved with them and failed. But when he crossed back into Country A, he had brought with him some of the disagreeable attitudes that he had picked up in Country B, so that he was now shunned in Country A. Until he resolved that life would be one long battle and sharpened up his skills to live in Country B or resolved to return to his considerate ways and resume residence in Country A, he would continue to have difficulties — he would be comfortable nowhere.

Mr. P was laughing and smiling at this scenario. He acknowledged that his behavior had changed and that he did want to go back to the mannerisms of Country A. He became more pleasant on the ward and gradually the staff trusted him more and more, Finally he was discharged. This type of confrontation is not unpleasant to the patient. It reminds him of a better time in his life that he had forgotten and helps him to return to an old way of acting that was more successful.

I believe that the cognitive approach to a patient with this kind of problem gives the therapist unique tools and an active, optimistic attitude. From a rational emotive behavioral point of view, no matter how negative the patient's life may be it is clear that this way of living is not inevitable. The therapist can derive energy by seeing the patient as having fallen into a trap. Having argued himself into an uncomfortable position, the patient has not yet found the argument that leads out of it. This metaphor makes the therapist feel alert. The problem may have been going on for a long time, but that does not mean that it had to go on for a long time. It has continued because the patient did not find the way out, but as soon as the patient and therapist can determine which way is out, help may be in sight.

Chronicity has a social aspect to it. If a problem is fresh and new, everyone tries to solve it. If the problem is old, potential helpers lose confidence; they feel it would be naive to think they can succeed where so many others have failed.

I have met patients who are referred to as chronic who have histories of good functioning in adulthood that are discounted after a while because their recent functioning has been so poor. If their relatives are unavailable to corroborate their stories, sometimes their stories about their good functioning are no longer even believed. These patients are a lost human resource. They are very different from the patients who have never functioned well, but they will only reveal themselves to a therapist who they think will believe them. Be on the lookout for such patients. They are worth watching for.

7

Depression

This chapter gives an example of a depressed man who responded to medication but needed rational emotive behavioral or cognitive therapy to maintain his improvement. It also gives examples of depressed ideas in patients with diagnoses other than depression.

Depression is a problem for which rational emotive behavioral therapy (REBT) and cognitive therapy have long been recognized as effective treatment.

Depressed patients are preoccupied with self-reproaches of the form "I am a _____," or they think they have figured out that the world is not ever going to be a satisfying place for them because their spouse "is a _____" or "everyone nowadays is a _____." They may have frightened themselves by believing they "can't stand" a situation. Their intense interest in these thoughts and their ability to discuss them with the therapist make these patients a logical focus of attention for the cognitive therapist. They provide a rewarding opportunity to apply therapeutic skill. An initial interview with a suicidal patient that successfully challenges the thoughts upon which the suicidal wishes are based can lead the patient to become hopeful about treatment.

Nevertheless, the rational emotive behavioral or cognitive therapist intending to treat depression on an inpatient ward encounters several immediate problems.

Only a small percentage of patients are diagnosed as suffering from clinical depression.

Those diagnosed as suffering from clinical depression are being treated with antidepressant medication or electroconvulsive shock treatment, and the patients and staff may share the belief that this is all the treatment that these patients need.

There are many patients suffering from depressed ideation who are nevertheless described diagnostically as "not depressed."

I once encountered a patient, Mr. D, who was a good example of a patient diagnosed as suffering from clinical depression. Mr. D was a middle-aged man who looked very sad, but whose depressed symptoms had not caused him to abandon his everyday politeness, rationality, and well-groomed manner of dress. To the ward staff, such a patient is extremely welcome. The staff is burdened with the task of managing many patients whose behavior and medical status are difficult to control. They have to worry about older, frail diabetic patients who go off their diets and younger patients using illegal drugs and stealing money and clothing from other patients. Many of these problems are so thoroughly confounded with the patients' background, character, and history that medication can no longer be considered a complete solution. When, in the midst of all this chaos, the staff gets a middle-aged man on the ward with no previous psychiatric hospitalization and find that he is suffering from an uncomplicated depression, they are only too happy to have at least one patient on the ward who they know has an excellent chance of responding to medication.

The ward staff liked and trusted Mr. D, chatted with him in a sociable manner, and reassured him that he would feel better and better each day as his medication took effect. If I had not taken it upon myself to interview him in greater depth, no one would have referred him to a psychologist, and, because he was headed for an improvement in mood, the staff would have felt satisfied to simply offer him encouragement.

This strategy is certainly understandable in view of the monumental and diverse tasks facing the staff of an inpatient ward, but it could have had serious effects for Mr. D. A major research study a few years ago (Simons, Murphy, Levine, & Wetzel, 1986) showed that the one-year relapse rate of patients who were treated for depression without cognitive therapy was 66 percent, whereas the rate for patients treated with cognitive therapy was considerably lower — 28 percent.

When I interviewed him, I found that his life had changed in the time just before his depression, and the new stresses to which he had been subjected had altered the way in which he thought about himself. Mr. D's father had died, and he had acquired some new responsibilities that he felt inadequate to handle. His mother was extremely sickly and rather demanding; his father had had a talent for managing her difficult behavior that Mr. D did not share. He was concerned about her intruding into his family life with her very frequent telephone calls, which had greatly increased since his father's death. Mr. D was inexperienced in handling this kind of situation, and he was prone to several kinds of irrational preoccupations. It was hard for him to decline any of her requests without thinking "I am a terrible son." When he chose to grant most of her requests, he was prone to thinking, "I can't stand this," and "Now I am a terrible husband, because I am letting my mother disturb my wife and children." He became absorbed in these self-defeating preoccupations and became more and more paralyzed, so that he was capable of dealing with less and less of what was going on. After a while, he couldn't even cope with simple things, because once the process of increasing self-preoccupation begins and the person becomes depressed, he cannot handle even what would have been easy for him before.

If we analyze the situation, we can see some possible reasons why the probability of relapse might be higher if Mr. D is treated only with antidepressant therapy and not with cognitive therapy. Mr. D's antidepressant medication has the capability of restoring him to the state he was in before his father died, but there are two serious problems that would make it unlikely that he could maintain this good mood. First, he is returning to a situation that is highly stressful and for which he has still not developed the necessary skills. Second, if he has not made any connection in his mind between the self-defeating preoccupations that he had developed and the onset of his depression, he might now believe that, in addition to all his other problems, he has had the misfortune to suffer from a major psychiatric problem.

Imagine the conclusions that he is likely to draw as he begins his life again. Because he has not developed the skills to handle his mother's demands, her requests begin to pile up. He will begin to have some of the same thoughts that he had before hospitalization, such as, "I am a terrible son," or "I can't stand it." When he notices these thoughts, instead of being prepared to debate with himself about whether he really becomes a "terrible son" when he cannot keep up with his mother's requests or to challenge himself about whether he really "can't stand it," he may conclude that his pain is an inevitable part of his situation or a recurrence of his depressive disorder. If he starts to feel depressed again, he may be prone to what is called in REBT depression about his depression. He may begin to ask himself, "Why me? Why should I have to be depressed? I have enough problems already. I can't stand it."

If, on the other hand, this patient is given a thorough explanation of the cognitive view of depression, he will be much better prepared to face his new difficulties without relapse. Instead of believing that he has suffered two separate major misfortunes — the loss of his father and being struck with a mental disorder — he understands that his irrational exaggerations "I am a terrible son" and "I can't stand it" helped to bring about his depression. He is prepared to challenge the concept that there is a separate group of people called "terrible sons" and that he meets the membership criteria for this group. Instead, he tells himself, "I am doing quite a few things for my mother, I would like to do even more, and I'm working on it." He has a unified, integrative way of understanding all of his new problems and how he can cope with them. He understands that his father's death put him into new situations and that, in dealing with these new situations, he fell into some unnecessarily painful ways of thinking. He may feel that he has matured because he has been through a major life crisis and picked up some new tools. These will help him to reduce such unnecessary emotional pain in the future. He remembers his feelings of depression, but he is not prone to feel sorry for himself because he can see how these feelings came about. It makes sense to him why he suffered this episode of depression and why he suffered it at this particular time.

Understanding the cognitive basis for depression is very important even for the patients who seem to fit a purely biochemical theory of depression. I once treated a patient who had spent a considerable amount of time on a ward for depression research. He told me, "I have endogenous depression," and he believed that this meant that his mood could not improve. We talked about his own mood range from low to high and the average mood range from low to high. He had not understood that his own mood range, even if it were lower than the average, was still open to him. He agreed that he would be perfectly satisfied to achieve mood states that he knew he could experience because he had experienced them before. This gave him some hope of recovery.

Scholarly books on cognitive therapy are so cautious in describing the results that a new practitioner might be unaware that, occasionally, a patient can experience a rather startling positive mood reversal in a single session. A direct confrontation of someone's basic irrational beliefs is an amazingly powerful technique that many therapists are reluctant to try.

Sometimes the confrontation of a patient's assumptions, such as "if someone has more money to spend on their children then he is a better person," leads to an inspired quasi-religious kind of feeling in the patient that may seem embarrassing to a self-conscious therapist.

I once talked to a young, unmarried mother of seven children who had the idea that she was a bad mother because she had failed to provide them with a house where they could all live together under one roof. Several of her children were living with relatives and this situation continually upset her.

When I challenged her belief that a house was essential and was a criterion of a good parent, her situation suddenly looked different to her. She was overcome by a feeling of being lucky that she had so many children and fond relationships and that all of her children were being well taken care of by her family. She was not simply transformed from being depressed to being calm and logical; she became absolutely radiant. Suddenly, money seemed unimportant to her compared to just being with her children.

In a way, it is not surprising that cognitive therapy should have this effect. The challenging of the materialistic is a basic tenet of most religious faiths. Believing in a spiritual world frees the individual from the tyranny of the absolutes of materialistic values. When these materialistic values are directly confronted, a certain euphoria is produced, even without any reference to an alternate, spiritual realm. Do not be embarrassed if a patient emerges from your office looking like she just came out of a revival meeting. This does not mean that you have departed from your therapeutic role. You have simply confronted some basic beliefs that were making the patient feel as if she were in a strait jacket, and she is feeling the effect of greater freedom. If you have stuck to the elegant solution of confronting irrational beliefs, you are on solid ground. The weakening of these irrational beliefs may create a positive effect that may endure a considerable length of time beyond the patient's initial euphoria. If, on the other hand, the patient seems euphoric because you focused on inelegant solutions such as praising her or predicting that she will get what she wants, there will be no positive effects other than a very temporary feeling of well-being.

For patients suffering from clinical depression, then, the cognitive therapist's role on the inpatient ward is to see that the improving patient understands the cognitive basis of depression. She will improve even if she does not understand this, but the understanding of this principle will help to prevent relapse. Even for patients who improve as a result of medication or the extra emotional support that hospitalized patients sometimes receive, some instruction in cognitive principles may help to prevent recurrence.

The cognitive therapist on an inpatient ward will notice that, in addition to patients diagnosed as suffering from depression, there are many patients in other diagnostic categories who are suffering from depressed ideation. The improvement of the depressed ideation will help them to recuperate from their illness, whatever it may be, to cooperate with the psychiatric team, and to make the adjustment of leaving the hospital.

A patient can seem intensely gloomy at times and even talk about suicide without meeting the diagnostic criteria for an episode of depression. In informal discussions and team meetings, such a patient may be referred to as "not depressed." This practice can be confusing to the cognitive therapist. Depressive ideation in the absence of clinical depression is a good reason to try cognitive therapy.

The type of patient who currently gets a diagnosis of personality disorder is a good example. Often these patients have episodes of intense depressive ideation, during which they engage in self-abusive behavior such as suicide attempts. From a superficial point of view, they seem to recover rapidly from these mini-episodes of depressed ideation. They can be seen on the ward socializing, eating, sleeping, joking, and laughing. However, they do not forget about these painful episodes or about the dangerous behavior that they engaged in because of these painful thoughts. They are often afraid of getting involved in life again because they are afraid of a recurrence of these depressed thoughts.

The cognitive therapist who undertakes to work with a patient who has a personality disorder in an inpatient setting may have difficulty convincing a multi-disciplinary team that this therapy for these depressed ideas is justified. Because of the definition of clinical depression, such patients will be considered "not depressed." Unfortunately, I have seen many occurrences of a struggle between treatment teams and personality disordered patients that are based upon the definition of depression. The team (taking the patient's complaint of depression as meaning that the patient claims to be suffering from clinical depression as defined in the current diagnostic manual for psychiatry), upon finding out that the patient does not meet the criteria for clinical depression, sometimes perceives the patient to be "faking" or "manipulative" and challenges the patient's need for inpatient care. The patient, aware of her own terribly low level of outpatient functioning, does not understand the team's position and is driven to increasingly desperate attempts to convince the team that she needs help. The cognitive therapist may spend a large proportion of the time that she devotes to a certain case to liaison efforts between the patient and the team.

Schizophrenic patients also suffer from depressed ideation. There are many obstacles to living as a schizophrenic person and many special talents that they need to develop to overcome these obstacles. They often get discouraged and can talk about it in a manner that invites useful interventions. For example, they have to endure poverty, loneliness, the disappointment of their families, being excluded from most meaningful activities, the constant proximity of other disturbed patients, and the discomforts of medication side effects. Many of them have to endure legal entanglements having to do with charges that were pressed against them for actions that they took when they were ill. Many of them have guardians who oversee their use of money.

Practitioners who believe that schizophrenics have not developed the capacity for meaningful relationships and independence may perhaps believe that schizophrenic patients do not suffer from the absence of relationships and from their lack of independence as much as a normal adult would. Unfortunately, I do not believe that this is the case. In spite of the fact that many chronically schizophrenic patients who are hospitalized know that their chances of finding a stable relationship or a degree of control over their life circumstances are slim, they still crave these things. If they occasionally slip into thinking that they "need" much more than they have and "can't stand" their circumstances, a session of REBT can often help them to return to their more philosophic frame of mind.

Oddly enough, when schizophrenic patients talk about the hallucinatory voices that they hear, the utterances of these voices that they find the most painful seem to be a collection of irrational thoughts from the pages of an REBT or cognitive therapy textbook. It is comforting to the patients who have to endure these voices to learn how to ask themselves questions that will make the messages of these voices sound less convincing. If the voices say "you are a failure," the patient who learns to think "is there really such a thing as a failure?" has taken a large step toward emotional recovery.

8

Images and Stories

The chapter discusses using rational emotive behavioral or cognitive therapy to help patients with negative emotions associated with frightening images and dreams. It also discusses using humorous images to help angry patients.

Many people believe that rational emotive behavior therapy and cognitive therapy are dull, dry, verbal, and technical and that, therefore, they cannot alter the patient's emotions.

I believe that this view is based upon a misunderstanding of the scope of cognitive and rational emotive behavior theory. It is true that a cognitive therapist can accomplish a lot by helping the patient to make modifications of his beliefs that can easily be expressed in verbal form; for example, changing "should" statements to "wouldn't it be nice if" and "I must" to "I sure would like to." However, the most basic principle of cognitive and rational emotive behavior therapy — that it is what the patient is thinking that affects his emotions (rather than outside events) — includes the patient's images and fantasies as well as the patient's abstract beliefs. Many of the patient's abstract beliefs are actually based upon some image that the patient has about himself, others, or some event. When these images are discussed, the patient can reevaluate his belief more effectively.

There is something very powerful about images and stories. Singer (1974) points out that the use of images seems to be common to many otherwise very different theories of psychotherapy.

Images, dreams, daydreams, and unusual actions need not be excluded from cognitive therapy. These are a part of the patient's thinking process. I am not suggesting an eclectic approach. I am not saying that cognitive therapy needs to be supplemented or watered down by some focus on fantasy. What patients have to say when they talk about their dreams and fantasies is some of the strongest confirmation for a purely cognitive approach that I have come across. The patient's dream or daydream is part of the process of pondering about what is wrong with him or part of his attempt to understand what is happening to him. It can be understood purely in cognitive terms.

Ms. Y, a young woman whose impulsive actions in the past had cost her the respect of her family, was talking to me about her efforts to repair her relationship with her sisters. One of her sisters had told her something that the other one had said about her. The patient felt devastated by the things they were saying about her behind her back. As she spoke, she used an image to describe how she felt. When her sister had told her about what had been said about her, she felt as if she were in a deep hole in the earth and her sister was shoveling dirt on top of her so that she couldn't breathe. What stronger confirmation could one hope to find of Albert Ellis's contention that many people feel that they need the esteem of others as desperately as they need air?

The patient's image gave me a good way to demonstrate to her that we react with our emotions to our image of what happened to us and not to what actually happened to us. She could see very easily that the panic she was feeling was appropriate to the situation of being in a hole and smothering rather than to the situation of being gossiped about by her sisters. She laughed with relief to realize that, no matter what her sisters said, she wasn't in a hole and could still breathe. The cognitive therapist is satisfied to demonstrate to the patient that her sister's esteem is not necessary to her existence. It doesn't matter to the cognitive therapist that the patient's metaphor for losing her sister's esteem was one of smothering rather than one of being attacked or drowning or in a fire. It doesn't matter how or when the patient acquired her stock of catastrophic metaphors. Once she acquires the confidence that she does not need someone's esteem (although she may want it), loss of esteem will no longer elicit a feeling of terror. The cognitive therapist's goal is not to explore the patient's catastrophic metaphors but to strengthen the patient so that these metaphors affect her feelings less frequently.

Freud emphasized that the psychoanalytic clients' thoughts about their dreams were part of the material that should be taken into account in dream interpretation (Freud, 1899). In cognitive therapy, these thoughts about the dream are also very important but for a different reason. For the cognitive therapist, the dream is an event like any other event that happens to the patient. The thoughts about the dream are the patient's beliefs about the event. When a patient reports that a dream has had a powerful effect on his emotions, the cognitive therapist will help the patient to see that it is not the dream itself that affects his emotions so powerfully but his beliefs about the dream.

One of my patients, who had grown up as an orphan, told me that he occasionally had a frightening dream of being lost in the forest. The confusion of his current situation was apparently triggering this nightmare often, and he was having it every night. Our discussion was an uncomplicated application of cognitive principles. He thought about what the dream meant to him — he articulated it as an indication that he was completely helpless. He thought about what to say to himself about that. He assured himself that he was grown up now and that he knew how to orient himself in the forest and find his way out. He was no longer a helpless child. After this brief discussion, he reported the next day that he had had his first night of uninterrupted sleep in a long time.

A veteran told me about vivid dreams of combat experiences from which he awoke terrified, sweating, and shaking. It takes a while for someone to get started talking about these kinds of dreams, and when he does, the conventional therapeutic hour is almost over. However, once the process of relating a dream gets started it takes a long time and is hard to stop. If the therapist can arrange to be available for a longer session than usual, it will provide an opportunity to discuss the patient's beliefs about the dream.

When I asked my patient what his thoughts were when he awoke from these dreams, he told me that he thought, "Oh no, I'm having flashbacks and I can't seem to stop. This means that I'm one of those veterans who has post-traumatic stress syndrome. This means that the next thing that's going to happen to me is that I'll be firing off a gun on a street corner because I'll think I'm in Vietnam."

By sharing the cognitive view of his experiences with the patient, he can become more confident about self-control. This view of traumatic processes is currently being developed by a number of investigators (see Ellis, 1994; Meichenbaum, 1994; Resick & Schnicke, 1993). The patient could see that it is very logical for the brain to store frightening memories and trigger them at times because of current experiences. The patient could also see that the most alarming thing about his dream was not the thought of undergoing the dream again, but the fear that it would lead to violence. He realized that in order to get from his bed to the street corner he would have to go through a series of steps that he could avoid. He began to see the dreams as a painful but understandable recurrence of frightening memories and physical sensations, rather than as a loss of control that would eventually rob him of his sanity.

If a patient can adopt a view of cognitive processes in which he can manage even his most painful emotional experiences by actively trying to soothe himself, then he will eventually learn to say to himself, something like, "Oh no, I am having another one of those painful flashbacks. What a terrible shame that I should have to endure these so long after I have returned. But I am going to comfort myself by relaxing, walking, reading, having a hot drink, or talking to somebody about it."

If the patient is one of those individuals who continues to feel bitter about the experiences leading to his dreams, some cognitive therapy for anger is needed. A person who is still angry about an injury has mixed feelings about allowing it to heal because he feels that his own suffering serves as an accusation to those who may have caused the injury. He perceives allowing his suffering to heal as letting the responsible parties off the hook. He perceives it as follows: "If I cease to suffer, then this injury wasn't such a big deal in the first place, and instead of other people being responsible for the pain I have suffered, it was I who was in the wrong for making such a big deal about it."

It often helps the patient to distinguish between the painful emotion of anger and the conviction that what was done to him was wrong. The emotion of anger and the experience of flashbacks are entirely private experiences, and if these painful experiences were to cease it would not prevent the patient from continuing to express his convictions about whatever injuries he feels were perpetrated upon him. Whether he is continuing to experience inner pain is not a public matter, and he does not have to tell anyone if he is still experiencing pain. Far from leading him to desert the other sufferers with whom he feels solidarity, a cessation of his own symptoms might give him more strength to comfort others or advocate their cause.

Anger has a kind of quasi-delusional component to it. When someone is angry, he often has an illusory feeling of accomplishment, as if his inner emotions were somehow righting the wrongs that had occurred. In order to allow himself to heal, he needs to give himself permission to stop being angry. It is often helpful to give the patient a larger perspective of the whole span of human history to help him forgive himself for being unable to correct the wrongs with which he is concerned. I found that several patients seemed to benefit from a general discussion of how wars and all of the outrageous things that occur in wartime have always been a part of human history, and the best minds have been unable, as yet, to think of ways to overcome this. Whatever their participation was in these wartime experiences, many others have shared this without ever having asked to be in these situations, and they have a right to try to heal themselves as well as they can. If some symptoms remain, they can at least not feel so angry about this, since it is not so easy, in our imperfect world, to go through life without acquiring some painful scars. It is not as if they barely missed living an entirely painless existence. Having some scars shows that they are living fully and have the sensitivity to respond to events that are painful. If they learn how to comfort themselves, this will strengthen them for other life experiences as well.

Painful recurrent images are not always flashbacks of past experiences, but can be imaginative constructions that have some value to the patient. I once saw a hospitalized patient for a few sessions who told me that he was an alcoholic and had been drinking steadily and frequently driving while intoxicated. He asked if I could help him with a recurrent frightening image that he had of being in a terrible car accident. I declined to try to cure him of this problem and explained to him that this image was his own way of trying to inspire himself to do something about his alcoholism.

Images can be a tool in the hands of the therapist who is trying to help a patient take her anger less seriously. One patient was angry about being unable to influence court proceedings in which she was involved. Because she could so easily visualize the proceedings going her way, she felt extremely frustrated when they didn't, as if she had been assured of success and it had just barely slipped out of her grasp. Invisible barriers are hard to accept.

"You could no more get those papers the way you want them than you could lift an elephant," I said.

For some reason, this kind of comment produces relieved laughter. Certain things just aren't possible, and if that is the case, it's a relief to accept it and to realize it wasn't some detail about the way you handled it. It just wasn't going to happen no matter what. An image often gets this across.

Patients' understanding of the inevitability of natural processes is a good metaphor for helping them cope with frustrations caused by people. Patients frustrated to the point of anger by the actions of other people sometimes react with amusement when asked if they get angry about rain or earthquakes. They come to realize that they expect the natural world to follow certain principles but that somehow they often expect people to transcend their limitations and imperfections.

Visualizing plants growing is a way of creating an image that helps to increase tolerance of delay. For example, hospitalized patients must endure long waits until their discharge planning process can be completed. Numerous details, all out of their control, must be handled before the social worker can finally offer them a placement somewhere. If, in spite of their assertiveness in reminding the social worker about their situation and the social worker's assertiveness in calling people on their behalf, things do not develop quickly, a metaphor from the vegetable world may have the desired calming effect.

"If you are growing corn and you want it faster, will it help to stamp on the ground?" I ask.

The patients look amused and often feel relieved of the burden of trying to push a process faster than it can go.

Visualizing exotic situations can often help patients to change their expectations. Often patients are angry about having to conform to regulations that they consider arbitrary, such as having to obtain certification to work at a certain job that they already know how to do. I ask the patients to imagine that they are on another planet and some little green men insist that in order to get something to eat, they must wear a purple robe and stand in a little circle. Often, the same people who are angry about some requirement here on Earth state easily, looking amused, that of course they would stand in the circle. Then it becomes clear to them that when they visualize themselves on another planet, they can go along with anything because they have no expectation that things will make sense. Here on Earth, however, they do have this expectation, even though it is frequently unjustified. When they drop this automatic expectation, they are able to handle arbitrariness with greater peace of mind.

When people visualize images, they often relax and their sense of humor is activated. In this frame of mind, they can see a disagreeable situation in a different light. Moreover, images are easier to remember than a series of verbal coping statements, and when they are remembered, the patients can use them to regain their perspective.

9

Work and Goals

This chapter gives examples of how the opportunity to work or to do something purposeful is critical to maintaining wellness for certain people. The therapist can use this principle to help patients regain a constructive focus.

Early in my training as a psychologist, I was assigned to a very psychotic patient. He almost never looked at anybody, and, when he did, he glared. He even sometimes made frightening, growling noises. His chart was anything but reassuring. It stated that he had been hospitalized more than 30 times and that he had struck his previous therapist. I was somewhat frightened of him at first, but it turned out that I had nothing to worry about because he never kept his appointments with me. Finally we developed a pattern where I would go and remind him of his appointment five minutes before it started so that he would remember to come. I don't remember helping him in any way during those brief sessions. For me, it was an opportunity simply to observe the process of a psychotic person getting well again. He gradually became more and more polite and cheerful and began to read the morning newspaper, until finally he was impossible to distinguish from any other good-humored senior citizen. He explained that he had faithfully taken his medication before he came to the hospital, but that he felt his routine had been disrupted by bad weather, which had kept him from going out and sitting on his favorite park bench and talking to all his friends.

I asked him what had helped him recover.

"Oh, I've been through this a lot," he explained to me. "The doctor does about 10 percent and the other 90 percent is up to me."

I asked him what he himself was able to do to get himself out of his illness.

"Well," he said, "I get myself interested in something. This time, I got interested in going to see my brother for Christmas. It kept me busy just making sure that I talked to people about getting a pass for the holiday, and it helped me to get myself organized."

Later on, I witnessed many other examples of rapid improvements in patients who had an opportunity to do something they perceived as purposeful. For example, one young man was selected to participate in a federally funded sheltered work program. He had to undergo a lot of testing to make sure that he was eligible. Finally the day arrived when he could get dressed up in the morning and leave the ward to go to work. An enormous change took place in his demeanor. There was a quiet, contented gleam in his eye, and he stood straight, tall, and very proudly. Six or eight weeks went by uneventfully, and he cheerfully went to work each day. One day, however, I noticed a change for the worse. He looked disheveled and restless and told me that he had started hearing abusive voices again yelling loudly at him. What had happened? The program had ended. He completed his last day's work, and immediately after returning to the ward the voices started again.

According to Albert Ellis, mental health is not simply the absence of irrational thoughts; happy, psychologically healthy people have goals that are important to them. They work hard toward achieving these goals and maintaining them. People become distressed when they are frustrated in an important goal; people who have a biological tendency to become mentally ill may be less able to tolerate such frustration.

As long as his work program was going on, the young man had a goal. Each day he could concentrate on getting ready for the next day. However, as soon as it was over, he no longer had a focus for his attention. Given his biochemical handicap, this lack of direction may have been too much for him to withstand without becoming ill again.

In one of the Veterans Administration hospitals they had work details that were available as patient activities — for example, a metal shop, an electronics shop, a printing shop, and a medical patient escort service. It was amazing to see the rapid improvement that took place in some patients when they were permitted to engage in these activities.

One exceedingly depressed patient was given an opportunity to earn a small amount of money by doing some piece work in one of the shops at the hospital that occasionally was able to get special contracts performing work for an outside business. His mood changed virtually overnight. He was very excited about this opportunity and tried hard to earn as much as possible.

Not only did I witness improvements in patients when they encountered a work opportunity, I also found that, in unravelling the history of psychotic people it often happened that interruptions in their work life were critical to their deterioration. For example, one man told me about a bitter experience in his life. He was a handyman, and someone had broken into his garage and stolen all of his tools. He had never replaced them, and was, thus, unable to continue working as he had before. Not only was the cost of the tools prohibitive, but every time he thought about buying new tools, he became angry and thought about how he "shouldn't" have to buy them because he had already owned tools.

Another had an excellent work history up until the time when he had developed a medical condition that prevented him from working. Not only did he have to stay at home, but he had to elevate his legs for much of the day. He fell into a state of depression, feeling like a complete burden to his family. When these feelings were discussed, he decided to do something useful for the family, and he took up cooking. Even though he could not stand on his feet for very long, he could do it long enough to cook good meals for the family. He once again felt useful.

One patient had a good work history until he learned some details about the personal life of his employer of which he didn't approve. He felt unable to continue working for his employer, so he left his job. He bounced from one interest to another and never settled down again.

Another had been working successfully for a number of years in a professional field for which he did not have the proper credentials. His company undertook a thorough audit, and he anticipated that his lack of credentials would be discovered. He also had some anxieties about his health. He left his job and embarked upon a sort of alternative, daredevil, counterculture lifestyle that he continued for a number of years. It was only when I went over his work history with him that he revealed that he had at one time had a good work record and that he actually still had an affinity for the sort of work that he had left. He sought some reassurance about his health problems and completely changed his demeanor after this — he started wearing a shirt and sports jacket and soon located a job where the employer knew about his lack of credentials but was willing to employ him anyway. He was soon discharged after several years of hospitalization.

One employed patient who had been repeatedly depressed was having marital difficulties. Upon exploring his history, I found that he had been involved for many years in volunteer work and had taken great pride in this until an organizational shakeup had changed his volunteer position. It was his disappointment with this situation that had led to a general feeling of discontent and caused some difficulties in his marriage. When he was able to realize that this event had in fact been very important for him, he and his wife stopped attributing his depression to marital difficulties. This led to an improvement in the marriage.

One highly intelligent patient who had worked for a successful company had some psychotic experiences and left his job. He wandered around the country and, by doing so, lost his possessions. After he became lucid again someone gave him a somewhat low-level job to help him out. It was not challenging to him, and he became severely depressed. He remained lucid while in the hospital and took on some complex and challenging volunteer assignments and some self-initiated study projects. These enabled him to get his mind operating at the level of complexity and speed that he seemed to need in order to feel good. He eventually made contacts in the community and found employment that was more suited to his level of intellectual intensity. When I questioned him about the time just before he had his psychosis, he revealed that, although his division in his company had previously always been busy, it went through a period of idleness that was hard for him to endure. There was also a certain amount of cover-up of this idleness with which he was expected to comply. Although he had not lost his job, he had lost his work and the atmosphere had changed.

One patient that I met on the locked ward told a story of woe. He told our team that he had once had a job, a car, and a wife. The wife left him, taking the car. He pursued her in order to get back the car. Because of his unplanned absence, he lost his job. Having lost his job, he could no longer make the car payments, and he lost the car as well. Since then he had become a wanderer.

One patient had worked for many years at a part-time job. Because of a lowering of his disability payments, he was no longer able to work only part time and tried working full time. He was not able to do this, became psychotic, and was hospitalized. I contacted his employer and was impressed to learn that, as a part-time worker, he had been the best worker the employer ever had.

What can we conclude from this collection of stories?

Intuitively, we might imagine that, with a cognitive handicap, an individual might have trouble doing a job. We might also imagine that someone with chronic emotional difficulties would have trouble behaving appropriately in a complex work environment.

Although these assumptions have much truth to them, in practice it seems that, for many individuals, work was an area of strength rather than something that taxed them. Often they demonstrated surprising stamina and devotion. A secretary once told me a story of something that had occurred in an office where she had worked. Her boss had interviewed a number of people for a job. One of them was an unfashionably dressed mentally ill woman who, when asked why she wished to work for them, admitted that it was because her mother wanted her out of the house during the daytime. Her boss chose another candidate who, at the last minute, was unable to take the job. Having other things to do, the boss delegated the choice to her secretary. The secretary chose the mentally ill woman just because she liked her. The most fascinating part of the story is that the woman worked for them for ten years and was one of their best employees.

To summarize, in focusing upon the work histories of my patients, I found that they often reported that they had had the ability to work very hard, sometimes even unusually hard. They seemed very hurt when these work involvements were ended, either because of factors related or unrelated to their psychosis or other personal characteristics.

I had the impression that many of these people, because of a tendency to psychosis, actually needed ongoing work and strongly felt, clearly understood commitments to keep themselves organized. They found it hard to endure being unoccupied without becoming confused or agitated.

In several of the stories I have related about patients' work histories, there was a rather sudden exit from a situation that had previously seemed stable and satisfactory. It might be natural to assume, for example, that the sudden disillusionment with the employer or the impulsive trip to find the automobile were merely early signs of impending mental illness and that the aimlessness that followed was a manifestation of the same illness. Unfortunately, these assumptions might lead a therapist to be discouraged about discussing the topic any further.

If, however, the therapist interprets the situation as follows, there may be more hope of a therapeutic dialogue. Assume that although the impulsive actions and the aimlessness may both be related in some way to the patient's mental illness, they are separate from each other. The patient may be unable to change the intensity of the feelings that lead him, on occasion, to make impulsive decisions and gamble his security on matters of principle. He may also be unable to widen the range of possible situations that would please him or that he could handle because his interests may be very intense and narrow. However, even given these problems, it is not inevitable that his aimlessness should last indefinitely.

The patient, from his point of view, has lost a situation that was very important to his mental health. It is best to acknowledge that he is in a dry spell and will need certain skills to help himself stay well during such a time in his life. These skills include:

keeping himself organized by temporarily replacing the major commitment he has lost with a number of minor commitments or routines that he can develop,

learning not to think of his work status or other achievements as a measure of his own worth, and

learning how to remain hopeful about finding more exciting things to do as time goes on.

I have found that certain patients are not likely to be satisfied with simply getting out of the hospital and living in a room somewhere. They may have worthwhile personal goals that seem to them very difficult to achieve, but sometimes the very fact that a goal is difficult can lead to greater inspiration to reach it. If the therapist can help the patient feel hopeful and not be easily discouraged, the difficulty of the goal can become a mental health asset rather than a liability because a difficult goal lasts longer and can provide a more lasting feeling of goal orientation.

The therapist might say, "Yes, it may be hard for you to find friends who see life just the way that you do, but there are so many people in the world, if you keep looking and looking, don't you think you'll find somebody that understands you better than some of the people you know now?" The therapist could also say, "Yes, it might be hard to find a volunteer job where they understand that you have to take so many sick days, but if you keep looking around, you might eventually find something. It might take a long time, but it might be worth waiting for."

The ordinary therapist cannot, of course, create employment or social opportunities for her patients. However, in addition to offering encouragement to the patient for the future, understanding the value of work and goals can give the therapist new tools for interaction with the patient. Reconsidering his past work life in a positive light can do wonders for the self-esteem of a patient. I am not speaking of vocational rehabilitation but of work life as a topic that the therapist can use to get a patient talking about positive aspects of himself. Many of our patients have been very disappointed in their personal relationships but have had good work skills. This was an area in their lives when they were able to feel a part of something beyond themselves. On the job, they may have enjoyed a sense of competence, togetherness, and cooperation that they have been unable to match in their personal lives.

Sometimes the work situation was a one-of-a-kind opportunity that the patient understands may never recur — for example, working for just one person who liked him. In spite of this, it seems to do the patient some good just to visualize and to talk about what he did at work during a time in his life when he was able to work. I once treated a highly delusional patient whose serious, intense, and preoccupied demeanor became more animated and relaxed after spending some time describing how he loved to repair bicycles. Another patient, very sad about an injury that kept him from returning to a former job, enjoyed just visualizing it and talking about it until he became more able to appreciate the potential satisfactions of his current life.

Often the therapist can get new insights into the patients' personalities by hearing about how they felt when they were well. The difficulties that the patients had at work often were related to some of their strengths, rather than to their difficulties. One young man, who seemed at times very uncompromising and critical with others, told me about how he always became angry with the work performance of his co-workers. A discussion with the occupational therapist proved enlightening — she said that his work speed was incredibly fast, far beyond the average. This helped me to talk with him about his difficulties in a different way. He had imagined that others were unwilling to work hard; he had never considered that they were possibly unable to work as fast as he did.

Often, when a patient remembers the pleasure that he had in doing an activity in the past, it seems to put him into a constructive frame of mind, in which he is able to generate positive ideas about the future. Some patients are able to think immediately in terms of feasible activities that they have a chance of accomplishing in the near future, such as hobbies, volunteer work, or simply helping friends and family on an informal basis. Others may be inspired to try to advance themselves occupationally by going back to school.

Some mental health workers feel uneasy when a patient begins to talk about goals because they are concerned that the goals may not be feasible, even if the patient has had vocational evaluation and counseling and clearly has the intelligence and the skills appropriate to his goal.

Motivation is a somewhat mysterious process, and how you react to a patient who is inspired with a goal depends upon how you think motivation works. Some people imagine motivation as being something that involves the individual pushing herself to do something. According to this view, because the individual must make such an effort she must be very careful to have a relatively small goal to start with because reaching a big goal would involve too much work.

In my experience, the metaphor of being pulled seems more appropriate. The idea of a big goal gets someone inspired, and he has a burst of energy that seems to pull him. Consequently, he is able to accomplish a lot of smaller things. A young person with a history of being psychotic may dream of being a doctor. It might get him as far as the community college bulletin board, where he might find some activities that he could do right now. By the time he has to admit that he will never be a doctor, he may have accomplished enough to be satisfied. If, however, someone else decides to convince him that he will never be a doctor, he may never make it to the community college bulletin board.

A therapist can be absolutely open with the patient about the way in which this might work. Encourage the patient to keep the goal in mind and to appreciate that what is important is not whether he achieves it eventually but that it is a way of getting started. Patients are capable of understanding the complexities of self-management. Therapists are usually careful not to make decisions for patients, but other ward staff often feel responsible for helping patients to decide whether certain goals are feasible or not. It is not easy to be a psychiatric patient. Critical comments that others may have avoided mentioning under other circumstances are often mentioned, because people feel that a person who isn't doing well needs all the feedback he can get. For example, if a moderately successful person who is not mentally ill mentions some goal that he is statistically unlikely to attain people are unlikely to disillusion or discourage him. However, when a psychiatric patient announces that he would like to go back to work, he may receive more criticism than he can tolerate and give up.

The therapist can help the patient to maintain his motivation if she talks to the team about regarding certain goals as tentative but not impossible. The state of positive motivation that is achieved when a patient gets excited about a goal is precious because it somehow seems to help with recuperation from the psychotic process. Unless the patient's goals are completely absurd or destructive in some way, it is very worthwhile for the psychiatric team to do whatever it can to facilitate this healthy state of mind.

If the team goes to the opposite extreme and, rather than discouraging the patient, discharges him prematurely, the patient's motives may be insufficiently developed to truly succeed, and his hopes may be quickly crushed. Ideally, the team should allow the patient a period of encouragement, during which the patient can begin to think of helpful details, make arrangements, and get into a realistic state of mind before undertaking the difficult transitions that lie ahead of him.

II

GROUP WORKSHOPS IN A
MENTAL HEALTH CENTER

This section relates the story of how a workshop program was developed in an acute psychiatric inpatient setting and the techniques that were used to stimulate large group discussions with videotaped vignettes.

10

Planning a Multidisciplinary Workshop

A colleague was often disappointed because of the lack of opportunity to do individual psychodynamic therapy on an inpatient ward. "As soon as the patients are well enough to participate in therapy, they get discharged!" he would say.

After we got involved in doing educational workshops, he would complain of fatigue, but he would say, happily, "I feel useful."

It is up to the therapist on an inpatient ward to design an environment where as many patients as possible benefit from discussion of problems that are pertinent to their situations. It was my good fortune to work at a mental health center with colleagues who understood the difficulties of inpatient practice and were interested in creating a situation that would expose large numbers of patients to discussions that would be helpful to them.

As I remember it, the beginning of our workshop program was something that just happened. I was sitting at lunch with another psychologist, and we talked about some of the frustrations of the inpatient setting. We agreed that groups were critical to our work in an inpatient setting, where we had only two psychologists for 150 inpatients. The small inpatient groups that we were running, which averaged from three to eight patients, were good mechanisms for helping withdrawn patients to increase socialization. They were not, however, an effective medium for conveying some other kinds of insight and judgment that would help our patients to complete their inpatient hospitalization successfully and move on to community living and outpatient treatment.

Moreover, we were frustrated with the kinds of experiences that we had been able to provide for our students. We had begun our careers at an earlier time when patients stayed in the hospital a little longer, and we had the opportunity to interact with patients long enough to understand something about their experiences and way of thinking. It had been our good fortune to work with a few especially articulate patients who had helped us to learn our way around the psychological map of the seriously disturbed patient. We had been able to develop a repertoire of stories and explanations about human behavior that were helpful in explaining situations to our patients. Our students were not as fortunate. An acute psychiatric inpatient setting whose main purpose is evaluation and stabilization can be a very confusing and frustrating place for a student. I will never forget the astonishment of one intern who was asked to do a psychological evaluation. She was patiently administering a comprehensive selection of psychological tests, and, of course, she planned to devote a number of hours to considering the results and carefully writing a report that she hoped would give the staff some insight into the patient's psychological needs. She was startled when, during her testing session with the patient, the sheriff came with a set of handcuffs and returned the patient to jail with his evaluation only half completed. The psychology interns' experiences with therapy were, unfortunately, also brief. Interns were frequently disappointed when their patients were discharged very soon after they began working with them. If we wanted our interns to come away from their internships with a sufficient number of experiences of doing effective psychological work with psychiatric inpatients, we were going to have to create an environment in which these productive interactions with psychotic patients were facilitated and occurred more frequently, instead of being a treasured, special experience.

Our situation was actually very favorable for creative change. We had a few psychology interns and some nursing and social work graduate students. We also had some video equipment that had been given to us by the volunteer department.

We decided that we would begin to run a new, educational group that would have the following features.

It would be a large group. In order to maximize our chances of including patients who would be articulate and enthusiastic about the workshop and would help it to be an educational experience for all of those attending, we decided to draw the patients from all the wards.

We would focus on some of the experiences, feelings, and thoughts that almost all hospitalized patients shared — feelings of being misunderstood, puzzlement about being brought to the hospital, shame about having to depend upon others, and a feeling that the world is an overwhelmingly cruel place. Moreover, we decided that we would focus on the most critically desired patient behavior in the inpatient setting — preparation for discharge.

The workshop would not only cover certain topics but also illustrate a certain way of interacting. There is something special about a group that is convened solely for the purpose of examining and discussing situations and ideas. No one in the group feels pressured to reveal personal problems or fearful of group confrontation. Group members feel, instead, like people attending a conference — expectant and hoping to hear or discover something new. Because the purpose of the workshop is not to persuade patients of anything in particular, the atmosphere can be one of intellectual honesty. People relate as equals and the main attribute that is modelled is an attitude of intellectual humility in the face of life's complications. The group can share the frustrations and the satisfactions of examining issues together. Because we wanted the group to have the atmosphere of a professional conference, we planned the details of the workshop to resemble a professional conference in every way that we could; for example, we had name tags for everyone, breaks, and refreshments.

We would produce and use short videotapes in order to stimulate discussion. Many therapists attend workshops on various forms of therapy and learn things that are personally useful to them by discussing case material about other people. We believed that it would be possible to give patients that same opportunity to learn helpful concepts and discuss pertinent issues without sharing personal information with a large group by creating videotapes with fictional characters that the patients could discuss.

We would make the workshop long enough to make a substantial contribution to the patients' welfare. We decided upon an ambitious schedule, just like a professional conference. We planned the workshop as a three-day program, with sessions of one-and-one-half hours (with a break in the middle) for three days in a row.

We would make the workshop multidisciplinary. Members of other disciplines were invited to get involved in the production of the tapes and the running of the workshop.

The making of the videotapes, although time-consuming, was surprisingly easy and gratifying once we overcame our initial hesitation. We began with a meeting of interested staff and students around a conference table, and, although everyone was positive about the idea of making our own videotapes, there was a certain hesitation about actually beginning. There was some inconclusive discussion about whether scripts would be needed. Finally, I suggested that we leave the conference room and begin making tapes immediately, with the idea that we wouldn't necessarily expect to make a usable tape on the first try. After looking briefly surprised, everyone agreed that this was a good idea. We moved to another room and began.

The vignettes that we made during that first session did not turn out to be our favorites. They were used only briefly, but we learned a lot from them. The first and most important thing that we learned was that we had an excess of things to say. Mental health workers spend many hours of their day listening to patients talk about their unique set of circumstances and problems. Because of this experience, workers store up a lot of implicit knowledge that is hard for them to express in organized form but that becomes visible when given an opportunity to role-play in a small, congenial group. When we put two mental health workers in front of a camera to improvise dialogue, we were quite surprised at what happened. We expected a halting, stammering, stalled conversation, but the two characters came alive and had a long, flowing conversation that we thought was very dramatic.

We were eager to try again. We met in another session one evening for a few hours after work and made a few more vignettes. We felt we had enough to try our first workshop.

We were very excited. We had no idea how the patients would react to our materials. We imagined them laughing at certain lines that we thought were funny.

Organizationally, things were going well. We had talked with all the disciplines. We needed to collaborate with a lot of people and found them very willing. We were able to create a schedule that didn't interfere with other activities. The activity therapists were kind enough to let us hold the workshop in their area, and they gave us valuable assistance by sharing the names of the patients who were attending activity therapy whom they thought might be interested. The nurses on the ward also suggested patients to us and promoted the workshop on the ward.

We went around to each ward and talked to each person who had been recommended to us. We found that it was best to approach patients individually, because then, if one skeptical individual had a negative reaction, such as, "Oh I've been to those boring workshops before," his remarks would not discourage other patients from choosing to attend.

About half of the patients that we talked to were interested in attending. The psychiatrists reviewed the names and wrote orders for all patients whose attendance was approved. The nurses coordinated the patients' schedules so that they could attend and reminded them about the workshop. The volunteers prepared coffee and cake or cookies to serve during the break. There were also some volunteers standing by during the workshop. The area we were in was locked and all the wards were locked, so that if any patient needed to use the restroom or wanted to return to the ward, someone needed to accompany them. The volunteers publicized the workshop in their newsletter. Finally, the housekeeping staff coordinated with us so that no one would try to buff the floor in the workshop area during the program.

11

Workshop Procedures and Video Vignettes

My patient, Ann, had agreed to come to an educational workshop. When the time for the workshop arrived, I went around to the different wards to remind the patients who were interested in coming. When I found Ann, she was in the middle of an argument.

She was hollering something to a staff member, something like, "You all hate me. Where is my check? You must have stolen it."

I approached her, paying no attention to the argument, and softly reminded her it was time for the workshop.

"O.K. I'd like to come," she said, but then continued to argue.

"It's time to start," I reminded her again.

"O.K., in a minute," she said, and continued to argue.

"Can you stop arguing and come to the workshop?"

"Yes," she said.

"When?" I asked.

She smiled.

"How about now?"

"O.K." she said, and came with me, leaving the argument behind her.

She participated in the workshop cheerfully, asking questions and causing no problems.

It has been some years since that first workshop. My most vivid memories are of some of the chaotic things that happened that day — such as all the patients arriving late because of a mixup about who was going to accompany them from the wards — and of the enthusiasm that the patients and staff showed for our special efforts. Our attendance for the three-day program was approximately 20 for the first day, 12 for the second day, and 18 for the third day. For later workshops, we developed a one-day program and usually had between 15 and 22 patients for the program.

We quickly learned that, just as we had too much to say on the videotapes, the patients had too much to say about the videotapes. We adopted certain patterns of handling the discussion that enabled us to keep it going at a reasonable pace and in a logical sequence.

Before playing a videotape, we would freeze it on the first frame and introduce all the characters to the audience. We also said a little bit about who they were and what they would be doing on the videotape.

We would then give the participants a question to keep in mind during the tape. For example, we would say, "This man is playing the part of a psychiatrist and this woman is playing the part of a patient. While we are watching, keep in mind, what is the main topic that she is trying to talk about, and what is the main topic that he is trying to talk about?"

We would not let the tape run for more than a few minutes without stopping for discussion. In the beginning we made tapes that sometimes ran as long as 10 minutes, but we discovered that after 2 or 3 minutes some of our more talkative participants were eager to begin discussion and could hardly pay attention to the rest of the tape. We began making the tapes shorter and shorter, and some of our later tapes lasted less than a minute. However, by stopping the tape in the middle for discussion, we continued to use the longer tapes that we found were popular with the patients.

During the discussion we summarized each participant's answer in a very short phrase and displayed them all on an easel pad. This practice served a number of functions. It encouraged us to make sure that we understood each participant's reply, it helped participants to understand each others' comments, and it was rewarding to the participants to see their comments recorded. It also exposed the participants to more lucid ways of expressing the same points that they had sometimes expressed in extended or rambling form.

If a patient began telling long personal stories, we emphasized that, although we would like to talk at length with each individual, our purpose for the workshop was for all to talk together about the characters on the screen. If we could, we abstracted something from what the patient had said and related it to the character on the video screen. The participants were made to feel welcome to talk to us afterward about any personal issues.

We made arrangements to take participants who wanted to leave back to the ward. Our model of a professional conference was helpful to us in deciding to allow the patients to leave at any time. At a professional conference, anyone may leave at any time with no questions asked. Patients have a variety of good reasons for leaving a group. For example, they may have medical appointments, family visits, or suffer from medication side effects. Our purpose was to keep the discussion running for those patients who were available to hear it. We did not feel that the atmosphere we wished to create, where willing participants comfortably exchanged information and ideas, was compatible with the idea that they couldn't leave at will. Also, our time was limited, and we did not want to use it in attempts to persuade people to stay when they wanted to leave.

Our workshop program became very popular with the staff and patients. We found it a challenge to find the time and energy to conduct these workshops, but we continued to do so for as long as we worked at the mental health center. In retrospect, we felt that making our own videotapes to use in the workshop enhanced the experience for all of us, and we felt fortunate to have the opportunity to do so. The patient population of each mental health facility at any particular time is unique in terms of their characteristics. How chronic are the patients? How old are they? What are they primarily concerned about? What is their educational level? Knowing our patients, we were able to create tapes from which we thought they would benefit. Knowing that these tapes were to be used only by ourselves for our patients, we did not feel too self-conscious when we acted in the tapes. We also did not have to worry about the needs of some other potential audience at another mental health center. Having used our own creativity to make the tapes, we had a certain eagerness to show them and to find out how the patients reacted to them. Finally, the patients enjoyed identifying us as the actors and actresses on the tapes.

Of all of the vignettes that we produced, there were a few that became our favorites that we used over and over again.

OUTPATIENT AND PSYCHIATRIST

The Videotape

A woman who has recently been discharged from inpatient care has her first meeting with her new outpatient psychiatrist. She has been looking forward to the meeting. She has had a pretty good week-and-a-half outside the hospital, except that when she tried to go shopping with a friend, her feelings were hurt. Her friend seemed upset with her, but the patient didn't know why. She has already discussed the problem with her family — she wants to make some decisions about how to handle it — and the family encouraged her to discuss it with the psychiatrist. She is hoping that he will be able to help her to restore her relationship with her friend. The psychiatrist, although he listens politely to her opening comments about the problem, does not encourage her to tell him more and does not help her to develop her thinking on the matter. Instead, he keeps asking questions about medication, symptoms, and side effects. The patient answers his questions but politely keeps asking when she will have the opportunity to discuss her problem with her friend because she wishes to make her life even better than it is. At the end of the interview, the psychiatrist explains that he does not have the time to discuss this with her, but he refers her for a social work screening. He explains that he will continue to see her about her medication and that it will be up to the social worker to decide if she can have some sessions devoted to her problems in living. The patient grasps the different functions of the two team members and seems satisfied with the upcoming social work screening.

The Patients' Reactions

Although we tried hard to play the parts in such a way that both characters could be perceived as well-meaning, the patients tended to take sides with one character or the other. Both characters received withering criticism from those patients who sided with the other character. The psychiatrist was accused of being totally ignorant, and questions were raised about his medical education. The patient was accused of being inappropriate because she keeps trying to redirect the conversation instead of simply answering the psychiatrist's questions. It took some group discussion before the characters could be perceived as unintentionally working at cross-purposes.

We had designed the tape to explain the roles of the different professions in our local psychiatric outpatient follow-up settings. We also hoped that the tape would encourage patients to be assertive in seeking outpatient care. But we also found that the tape was useful when presented in a more general context, such as a discussion of feeling lonely or finding someone to talk to. The patient in the tape could serve as a role model for someone who has a certain topic that she wants to talk about. She tries very politely and accepts the situation of being unable to discuss what she wants. Nevertheless, she softly persists in asking for other opportunities to discuss the same thing. She is not insistent. She can wait. But she is determined to find someone to talk to. After viewing this tape, the patients were able to discuss the difficulties of finding people to talk to, different ways of going about searching for someone to talk to, and different ways of helping themselves to be patient until they could find someone. They also could discuss the more general topic of perceiving what is available from whom without being judgmental and tolerating disappointment.

EX-PATIENT AND HUSBAND

The Videotape

An ex-patient, whose husband expects her to keep up with a normal daily schedule of feeding the children and getting them off to school, tries to explain to him that when she is alone, she fails to focus on her daily tasks because she finds herself captivated by ruminations about "what are we all doing here?" and "do I have that funny feeling again that I'm not real?" He manages to convince her, by explaining the possible consequences of her not keeping up with things, that her tasks are important. What she finds even more encouraging, however, is that she realizes that he doesn't trouble himself about the cosmic questions that bother her. It is not as she thought — that the "normal" people have the answers to the riddles of existence. Instead, she realizes that the "normal" people know better than to expect to find the answers to these riddles. They are satisfied with much less — just to keep up with their daily existence. She laughs and says that will be easier than what she was trying to do before.

The Patients' Reactions

The patients enjoyed this videotape. Their discussions tended to focus on whether the husband's demands were reasonable and whether he was patient with his wife, but, in general, they seemed somewhat amused by the communicative encounter between someone who was focusing on normal life and someone who was focusing on profound questions that the other person didn't even understand. We used it successfully with the theme of "feeling less alone" as an example of people who feel alone because they think so differently. The conversation was an example showing that even people who think very differently can communicate if they are very patient.

IS THIS PATIENT READY TO LEAVE THE HOSPITAL?

The Videotape

This was a series of very short vignettes. In each one, the focus was on a patient trying to explain to his or her treatment team that he or she was ready to leave.

Overconfident

A young man states "I'm going to do great. I've been thinking about it. I can feel it," but when the doctor asks where he is planning to live, it becomes clear that, despite his confidence, he hasn't made any definite plans. All he says is "I've got contacts."

Lethargic

A woman is tired of her strenuous schedule of inpatient activities and is looking forward to going home where her husband will completely take care of her.

Accepting

A woman is going home to live with her mother. She mentions some restrictions that her mother will put on her activities. She doesn't really care for these restrictions, but she plans to accept them in order to live peacefully with her mother until she might be able to live on her own.

The Patients' Reactions

The first vignette was very successful in eliciting a lengthy discussion about what it takes to make a person ready for discharge, and we often didn't even have to use the subsequent vignettes.

We found that if we asked the patients whether the character was ready to leave, they were very reluctant to say no, almost as if they were being asked to judge him or her as a human being. However, if we asked them "in what ways is he or she ready to leave?" and "in what ways is he or she not ready to leave?" they were able to list many of the strengths and weaknesses in the character's state of discharge readiness.

THE OVERINDULGENT FAMILY

The Videotape

Five sisters and brothers of a patient about to be discharged make plans to take care of their brother's every need when he gets out. We portrayed the family as going to what we regarded as ridiculous lengths to protect their brother from any effort or emotional discomfort, such as taking off time from work to bring him a newspaper to read in bed, working in shifts to bring him meals in such a way that he didn't have to prepare them himself and also didn't have to be with anybody, inviting friends to come and keep him company who were informed that when he felt like being alone they should quickly disappear, and colluding with him to make it appear to his parents that he was applying for jobs.

The Patients' Reactions

We used this tape over and over again to stimulate discussion of issues concerning self-care and the degrees to which different families are willing to help. We were surprised to find that most of the patients did not find the tape as humorous as we did. They wistfully wished that their families would do as much. It took some discussion to bring out the viewpoint that some of the fictional family's efforts were excessive. Although patients didn't tend to laugh at the tape as we had hoped, the discussion using the tape was much less stressful than earlier discussions of family issues that we had attempted without this tape. Because the family on the tape was so incredibly solicitous, they didn't stimulate-highly charged memories of family problems as did an earlier tape that we had tried that portrayed a family conflict.

LIFESTYLES

The Videotape

Two brothers are shown on the screen back to back, each musing about how the other one has it better. The one who has been a psychiatric patient envies the success in school and on the job that the other one has enjoyed. The successful brother envies the free time and the spontaneity of the other.

The Patients' Reactions

Patients were genuinely surprised at the feelings of the successful brother. They commented very favorably about discussing this theme.

III

A SPECIAL TOOL FOR PATIENT EDUCATION

12

Creating and Field Testing the First Interactive Videodisc Simulation for the Chronically Mentally Ill

This chapter relates the story of the unique opportunity I had to produce and field test an interactive videodisc for the chronically mentally ill entitled, "How to Get Out and Stay Out: The Story of Cathy."

I was fortunate to have the unique opportunity to create a special tool for psychiatric patient education — an interactive videodisc called "How to Get Out and Stay Out: The Story of Cathy." This videodisc is currently being used in only a handful of mental health facilities, but it is an example of the sort of tool that could be used more in future patient education. I am setting down here some of my thinking about the purpose of the videodisc, the concepts involved, and the way in which it was created, because I hope others will also contribute to the creation of such tools. Those interested in finding out more about similar computerized tools that are available to use with the mentally ill can consult Barsh and Jackson (1996).

The idea of using interactive videodisc technology for the mentally ill grew out of my experiences with the multidisciplinary workshop at the mental health center. Although all of us who were involved in the workshops felt they were a worthwhile focus for our efforts, they tended to occupy us for an entire week, during which we would fall behind on the other, everyday, routine tasks of inpatient care, such as documentation. We could not commit enough time to expand the workshops into a continuous program. We were not able to offer it more than about once a month. However, the program was popular with the patients, and between sessions patients would ask when we were going to have another workshop.

I began to think about ways to offer patient education between workshops. I quickly realized that finding educational materials for the mentally ill was a challenging problem. Traditional films and videotapes require the viewers to sit through long portions that do not pertain to their own problems, thereby straining the low attention span of the mentally ill. Moreover, the content of any programming that is designed for a popular audience is not usually pertinent for the mentally ill. In fact, studies of television programming have indicated that the mentally ill are portrayed on television in a very unfavorable light (Gerbner, Morgan, & Signorielli, 1982). They are often portrayed as either violent or the victims of violence.

I considered using videotapes, such as the ones we had made for the workshops, but decided that, however brief and pertinent we could make them, these would probably not meet the needs of the patients nearly as well as the workshops. We had found that after even a few minutes of viewing a videotape, the patients had generated such a large volume of comments that some discussion was needed to help them focus. A videotape that patients could benefit from viewing independently would have to include two important components. First, the tape would have to include something like the vignettes that we had used for our workshops to capture the patients' attention and give them memorable models. Secondly, the tape would have to include something like the discussion of the vignettes that we had done at the workshop; in other words, some way of helping the patient to focus and assimilate something useful from the tape. I realized that a patient education tool like this would require a lot of time to design.

I was at this point in my thinking when I heard about an opportunity to work with a group devoted to mental health computer applications. I decided to leave my position in the psychiatric hospital and devote two years to being a postdoctoral fellow at the Missouri Institute of Mental Health. There I would be able to concentrate on developing a tool that could be used for patient education in mental health settings.

A new and outstanding teaching tool — the interactive videodisc — was just becoming affordable enough to stimulate interest in people like myself, who had educational goals in mind. The interactive videodisc was being described as a marriage between computers and video. By hooking up a computer and a videodisc player together, a teaching machine with new capabilities is created.

The videodisc has certain features that make it superior to videotape for teaching situations. With a videotape, you can use the fast forward and rewind controls to find the beginning of your educational segment, but should you want to show more than one of these segments on a particular occasion, you may have to stand in front of your group fast-forwarding and rewinding repeatedly until you finally find what you are looking for. The inexpensive videotape machines that we use in clinical practice do have counters, but they are not accurate enough or standardized enough to prevent you from having to make a last minute search while your group of patients begins to fidget. On a videodisc, however, each part of the video has a definite frame number, and the videodisc player can find any frame almost instantaneously.

When you freeze a videotape player on a particular frame so that your group can have a discussion, you may get static in the picture, and your machine probably has a feature that prevents you from freezing it for very long in order to protect the tape. With a videodisc, you can pause and the picture will be clear, and your group can discuss it indefinitely without harming the disc.

When a videodisc player is interfaced with a computer, a still more powerful tool is created. With a computerized videodisc, it is no longer necessary to make note of any frame numbers. A display on the screen offers you different options, and you simply note which one you want. You can do this by touching the keyboard or, if your interactive videodisc system includes a device called a touchscreen, you can indicate your choice simply by touching the screen. The videodisc player will begin playing the desired sequence almost instantaneously. The way in which people make their choices can be made very simple with a touchscreen display that includes large squares or pictures for them to touch, so that they do not have to focus on small keyboard devices. A videodisc program that has been computerized so that the viewer can make choices is interactive.

At the Missouri Institute of Mental Health, there was an interest in providing me with the training and support that I needed to produce an interactive videodisc for direct patient care. I was sent to a videodisc symposium and a videodisc production workshop in Lincoln, Nebraska, where the public television network and the university had collaborated on many successful projects and had created a center for videodisc production and training.

These workshops were tremendously exciting because of the enthusiasm and optimism about this new medium. I hadn't quite realized it, but I had become accustomed to a sort of dreary pessimism in the field of mental health. Funding in the mental health area was decreasing, and our programs always seemed to be shrinking. At the videodisc events, I found myself in a completely different atmosphere. Here were elementary school teachers, college professors, and corporate executives, all excited about the same new medium and all of the things that it could do for the people that they served. The excitement that people felt about the new medium was inspiring them to think big; they were planning ambitious educational projects that required the collaboration of large numbers of people and large amounts of funding.

The videodiscs shown at the conference were worthy of the excitement generated. Because of the capability of the videodisc medium to move quickly from one sequence to another, a simulation could be created where a continuous story unfolded, and the viewer could make choices for the main characters and influence the outcome of the story. I saw two simulations that inspired me. Both were designed for medical education. One was the story of an alcoholic who arrives at a hospital (Harless, 1986). The medical student viewing the videodisc decides what questions the patient should be asked and orders appropriate tests and treatment. Another was designed to teach emergency medicine (Henderson & Galper, 1987). It begins with a riveting scene of a very sick young man arriving at an improvised medical field station. The student watching the simulation has to respond correctly within a certain amount of time in order to help the patient.

I became thoroughly convinced that the simulation was the kind of design that I should use for my disc. I had always found that patients' attentiveness improved when I could tell them a story. I reasoned that an educational video based upon a story would prove more memorable than a video organized around a specific topic or skill. Because I was not sure if I would have another opportunity to make an interactive videodisc, I wanted to make one that truly demonstrated the unique contribution that the videodisc medium could make. Hopefully, later on, others would make additional discs about other characters and topics. I could envision an interactive videodisc system being used in a number of different ways on a psychiatric ward. I could visualize it in the dayroom, where any patient who wanted to could interact with it, or in the occupational therapy area, the patient library, or a special purpose room where different therapists could bring individual patients or groups.

When I returned from Nebraska, I spent about eight weeks writing the first draft of my script. There were certain things that I knew at the outset. I wanted to develop a believable main character, a fictional psychiatric patient who had the kind of psychotic symptoms and life situation with which patients could identify.

I wanted to focus on the critical theme of staying out of the hospital that we had focused on in the inpatient workshops; in fact, I decided to use a title that we often used at the workshops, "How to Get Out and Stay Out." I visualized the story beginning with a patient actually leaving the hospital, carrying all her belongings with her in a plastic garbage bag, as so many of the patients actually did.

There are indications in the research literature that stress may precipitate psychotic episodes in vulnerable individuals, but that this stress may be buffered by good social support and other factors (Zubin & Spring, 1977; Zubin, Steinhauer, Day, & van Kammen, 1985). I wanted to create a plausible dramatic illustration of the way in which this buffering could avert relapse. I wanted the character to encounter a problem, and I wanted to use the technique of interactive simulation to reveal an overview of the consequences of different ways of handling this problem. Some pathways through the simulation would show the character elaborating the problem further and further until she became distressed enough to begin to experience a relapse. Some pathways would show the same main character with the same problem successfully managing stress and remaining in good psychiatric condition.

I also wanted to demonstrate the cognitive basis of stress management. I planned to have the main character engage in varied methods of dealing with her problem, such as social support and relaxation, and show practical steps taken by the character to solve the problem. My goal was to illustrate that all of these varied methods had something in common; they all changed the way in which the character thought about the problem and the level of emotional intensity she experienced. This goal would be accomplished by having the character think out loud on the screen, so that the viewer could see how, in the presence of supportive others or in a state of relaxation, the character found new ways of thinking that could soothe distress about the problem.

First I planned a structure for the Cathy story. It was only later that I decided what her problem would be. I planned that whatever the problem would be, the viewer would have varied choices for self-help — people for Cathy to talk to about the problem, ways of thinking the problem over, ways of doing something about the problem, and ways of relaxing. I also planned that there would be a scoring system, so that whatever self-help the viewer selected for Cathy would add up. The score would be used to determine Cathy's level of freedom from symptoms. There would be a number of different endings, some with Cathy returning to the hospital and some with Cathy remaining in the community. At the end of the simulation, the viewer could choose to receive feedback about the choices that he had made (for descriptive details about the videodisc, see Olevitch & Hagan, 1989).

Finally, I decided upon her problem. I wanted it to be something fairly innocuous, something that would not lead patients to think that they were so different from her that they couldn't learn from her experiences. I also wanted it to be only mildly stressful, so that the viewer would be in a calm state of mind and receptive to learning. I hit upon the idea of having her come up to a supermarket checkout counter and have trouble finding her money in a large, overstuffed purse, while the person behind her made impatient remarks.

After writing the first draft of the scenes, the process of working on the branching began. I was fortunate to have as my partner on the Cathy disc the research assistant at the Missouri Institute of Mental Health, Brian Hagan. Together we discussed all the different ways the viewer could move from one scene to another and the implications of each.

There were three main branches to the simulation. After Cathy was embarrassed at the checkout counter and emerged from the supermarket, the viewer was given a choice of whether Cathy should go back to the hospital or try to stay out. If he chose for Cathy to go back to the hospital, he went to the Immediate Rehospitalization branch, which was very brief, and ended with Cathy wondering whether she had given up too easily when she came back to the hospital. If the viewer chose to hear feedback, the narrator encouraged the viewer to try again and to keep Cathy out of the hospital longer.

If the viewer chose to keep Cathy out of the hospital, he was faced with his next choice — he was given a choice of responding yes, no, or don't know to the question, "Is there anything Cathy can do to help herself?" An affirmative response to this question put the viewer into a branch of the simulation called Self-Help. In this branch there were ten different self-help options. These self-help scenes show Cathy thinking her problem over, having conversations with others about it, getting organized, enjoying relaxing activities, and so on. In each scene, she succeeds in helping herself to feel better about what happened. After each scene, the viewer was asked "Is there more Cathy can do to help herself?" If he replied yes, he was returned to the Self-Help branch to continue making selections.

If, when Cathy emerged from the supermarket, the viewer chose no to the question about whether she could help herself, he entered the Rumination branch of the simulation. The Rumination branch begins with Cathy sitting alone and beginning to elaborate her problem, "what kind of a woman can't even hold on to her own purse?" and "the nerve of that man behind me." There is only one opportunity for Self-Help on the Rumination branch — the possibility of having dinner with a fellow boarding home resident.

After the viewer has either left the Self-Help branch or the Rumination branch, there is one more opportunity for self-help — the viewer has the option of reminding Cathy to take her medication. At the end of this choice, the choices for self-help made by the viewer are tallied. According to his score, it is automatically decided which of five different sleep scenes he should see, ranging from "sleeplessness — severe" (in which Cathy hears persistent and accusatory hallucinatory voices) to "sleep — great."

There are a variety of other scenes and choices that occur the next day and a total of eight different final outcomes, including the immediate re-hospitalization ending. In the best ending, Cathy returns to the store with her purse in hand and has a friendly conversation with the store clerk. In the worst ending, Cathy is hospitalized on the locked ward after going back to the store and causing an argument. In some of the in-between endings, Cathy stays in her room instead of going out, or she goes to the psychiatrist and is either readmitted for a brief time or re-ceives reassurance.

After the viewer has reached one of the eight different endings to the story, he sees a narrator who gives him the choice of hearing feedback about the ending that he reached. Then he is offered the option of hearing more feedback about his choices. If he selects this feedback, he hears first about any critical negative choices that he made, such as avoiding medication, and then about his other choices.

When we made decisions about branching, we had to decide the con-sequences of each of the viewers' choices. Should viewers who chose only enough self-help to prevent Cathy from hearing the worst voices see the scene where the psychiatrist readmits Cathy or the scene where he re-assures Cathy about remaining in the community? Should viewers who selected a lot of self-help but no medication be permitted to see the best ending? If the viewer selects for Cathy to have dinner with another resi-dent and take her medication, is that enough for Cathy not to hear any voices at all? After Cathy causes a big argument at the store, should we give her a chance to explain herself to the psychiatrist?

We also edited all the scenes, removing extra dialogue and thinking that was not critical to the scene. Scenes in interactive video have to be very short. At the time we made the videodisc, thirty minutes was the maximum duration of video footage that could be pressed onto one side of an interactive disc. Our story took about five minutes to develop to the point where the viewer started making decisions. We had ten self-help scenes and a variety of other scenes to include, as well as feedback and messages to the viewer who failed to respond. Consequently, most of our scenes had to be edited until they were less than a minute.

In a video that is not interactive, a certain number of transitional scenes must be planned, that is, small scenes in which characters enter or leave a room or pass through a doorway or up a flight of stairs. In an interactive video, the number of transitional scenes is even greater because the designers must anticipate all the possible paths the viewer might take through the simulation and make sure that there are enough transitions so that all of these paths seem smooth. Eventually, we spent quite some time outside the supermarket videotaping our main character coming in and out of the store and pausing or not pausing in either a happy, angry, or indifferent mood.

When it came to the production of the videotaped scenes, we were able to draw on a unique pool of talent. I had not only been inspired by my work at the mental health center to create the disc and given direction by the needs of the mental health center, I was also fortunate enough to have made the acquaintance of a number of the mental health workers who were willing to volunteer to be part of our acting staff. Our leading lady, Susan Reidhead, had been a psychology intern when I worked at the mental health center and had participated in the videotapes for our workshops. Even though she was now working full time, she agreed to help us. I was touched by the efforts that she and our volunteers made to help us complete our project. We met during lunch hours, on Sundays, and whenever we could wedge in a little production time without interfering with anyone's other responsibilities. This was time-consuming — it took us months to complete the production, but I had the time because of the Missouri Institute of Mental Health postdoctoral program. Thanks to the talent of our video technician, John Stalsworth, our video footage was expertly edited into a smooth, interactive story.

People in the community were also incredibly helpful. I found a real taxi driver to play the taxi driver, a real policeman to play the policeman, and a real boarding home owner to play the boarding home owner. A supermarket manager cleared a whole checkout line for us where we could produce the scene of Cathy fumbling in her purse. Some of the actors waiting in line behind her were supermarket employees who were permitted by the manager to volunteer.

After videotaping the scenes, it was time for them to be field tested. I returned to the mental health center where I had done the workshops and once again gathered small groups of patients to watch the video scenes. Although it would not be possible to take advantage of all of the special features of interactive video until all of our video footage was pressed onto a disc, we were able to present a scene with the choices that the viewers would have once the video was interactive. Then we could manually show another scene depending upon what the group wanted to see.

The field testing turned out to be a very rewarding experience. I had envisioned the videodisc primarily as a tool for individual patients to use, and I was surprised to see how well the scenes worked with a group. We would show a scene and then ask group members to discuss which choices they would make and what their reasons were. The group members were surprised at each others' choices and discussion was stimulated.

We were interested in whether the video would generate interest, which of several versions of instructions about how to operate the video would be the most successful, and whether the choices that we had designed were successful in generating a feeling of involvement in the story.

We saw immediately that we had succeeded in generating interest and holding the patients' attention. From the moment Cathy appeared, ready to leave the hospital with all her belongings in her plastic bag, the patients' eyes remained on the screen.

Our instructions, however, needed some work. We discovered that if we put the instructions at the very beginning, before the story started, by the time Cathy arrived at the first point where the viewers were supposed to touch the screen they had forgotten what to do. On the other hand, if we waited until the climactic moment when Cathy emerged from the supermarket to switch to a narrator talking about how to make a response, we lost our viewers. We had to redesign the instructions. We waited until Cathy emerged from the supermarket and then, leaving an image of Cathy pausing outside the supermarket on the video screen so that the viewer did not have to leave the story, we had the narrator give a much briefer set of instructions. This sequence was successful in getting the patients to make their choices by touching the screen.

The group meeting in which we tried out our choices proved to be unusually interesting. We showed the scene of Cathy spilling her purse at the checkout counter and then a scene of her beginning to think over this experience as part of helping herself. We posed the question, "Do clumsy people have to stay out of the way?" I held my breath as the group watched the scene and considered the question. Would the whole group find this choice so absurd that there would be no diversity in their answers? I had taken the idea for this question from my work with an individual patient who had the idea that, if you were slow, you were more or less obliged to stay out of the way (see Part I, Chapter 5, "Some Deviant Belief Systems," for more details). Would other seriously ill psychiatric patients find this idea plausible enough to choose yes as their answer, or were each patient's ideas completely different? Would it be possible to use the deviant thoughts of one patient to entice another into a discussion?

I was gratified and surprised to see that this answer was actually chosen by several members of the group. There were several women in the group who agreed that Cathy was actually dangerous to others because she was so clumsy. They speculated that if she were near some glass jars she could knock them over and hurt a child. They believed she should stay home.

A young man in the group, a different sort of personality from these women, was amazed by their timidity and set about convincing them in a very supportive way that Cathy had a right to go out. Everybody in the group had a good time. I concluded that it was indeed possible to use the thinking of some patients to structure programs for other patients.

Our experiences with the field testing were a confirmation of my deeply held conviction that the psychiatric patient is not unable to communicate but is simply handicapped at communication. When I was in college, I had a summer job working for a social agency that helped clients with cerebral palsy. Many of them had such difficulty articulating sounds and writing that their teachers had mistakenly concluded that they were unable to learn. When they were taught to type, however, they were able to reveal their skill at communication. The handicap that had devastated their motor skills was still there, but it had been bypassed.

The situation with psychiatric patients is similar. Patients cannot articulate their problems well enough in a group to get help in the way that therapists expect because they feel ashamed and they jump from topic to topic. By providing patients with a fictional character on which to focus, we provide a topic that will give them some of the same insights without a group member having to reveal his own situation. By using a medium that allows us to break down the action in the story into small segments and focus on them one at a time, we can facilitate a useful discussion among patients who might ordinarily jump around from topic to topic without completing anything.

The process by which we were able to revise our instructions until they were successful in getting the patients to touch the screen was very satisfying. We actually only revised the instructions once, but we were in a position to continue revising them until we were successful, because that was the task that we had set ourselves — to work on our program until it fit the patients' needs. I believe that if we commit more of our mental health dollars to permitting mental health workers to engage in work such as this, we will be buying something of lasting value. Because of the way in which our mental health centers are organized now, there is no one whose primary job is to do this sort of work, even though this kind of work is central to the purpose of mental health institutions. I believe that there are many mental health workers with the talent and motivation to engage in these tasks if given the opportunity.

Upon completion of our field testing, we edited all the scenes together onto a master tape and sent it out to be pressed onto a disc. I then wrote a computer program for it in BASIC. I selected this language because it is readily and inexpensively available for all IBM compatible personal computers. I used only the features available in this language. I did not use any special graphics cards or software that would require users to obtain a license. My hope in doing this was to make this technology accessible for mental health centers with ordinary levels of funding.

Having completed the videodisc, we were now ready to try it out with psychotic patients and evaluate our results.

13

Taking the Videodisc on the Road

This chapter tells how patients reacted to the Cathy story and its interactivity.

What was it like to show an interactive videodisc to our research subjects, who were all suffering from schizophrenic disorders? Some of our subjects were assigned to our experimental group and used the videodisc interactively for two sessions. Our control subjects were shown a few scenes and asked for their opinions about the video during two sessions as well. The detailed method and results of our experimental investigation can be found in Olevitch and Hagan (1991). Here I would simply like to share some of our experiences during the study.

It has already been documented in the research literature that psychotic patients can interact comfortably with computer devices (Greist, Gustafson, Stauss, Rowse, Laughren, & Chiles, 1973; Greist, Klein, & VanCura, 1973; Selmi, Klein, Greist, Johnson, & Harris, 1982). Nevertheless, we were surprised at the ease with which our subjects interacted with the Cathy videodisc. They were easily able to touch the screen to make their choices, and they did not express any surprise that this was possible or indicate that they found this in any way remarkable. Only one patient hesitated when the instructions to touch the screen were given. She sat there for a moment staring. Finally, I said, "go ahead," and she immediately began to participate. She knew what to do, but she was waiting for permission. There were some other patients who were talking to themselves while they watched the videodisc but were nevertheless able to make choices when the menus were shown.

There is a sequence on the videodisc that informs the viewers when they touch an inactive part of the screen and asks them to try again. This sequence was activated a number of times, mainly because of temporary malfunctioning of our touchscreen; our viewers repeated their choices and took this in stride. A few technically informed patients asked questions about the computer control of the videodisc, but mostly the viewers interacted with the disc without commenting on the technology.

We had absolutely no problems with any patient being fearful of the equipment or trying to damage it in any way. In spite of many skeptical comments from people that patients might interpret the program's interactivity in a paranoid way and react negatively, as patients do who think the television is talking to them, we had nothing occur that caused us even the slightest anxiety on this score.

The patients were polite and appreciative, and, when we encountered them in the hallways of the hospital on subsequent occasions, they sometimes made appreciative remarks about the program.

Over a year after the subjects had completed their interaction with the videodisc, I thought that I might have the opportunity to do a follow-up study. I began calling the subjects to ask if they remembered their experience with the videodisc. I never had the chance to complete this work, but I was encouraged to find that the subjects in the experimental group remembered many of the details of the Cathy story.

We tested a sample of hospital patients and carried our videodisc system to a series of residential care facilities in the community. This was my first exposure to community facilities, and I was fascinated by them. Some of them seemed a lot like hospitals, with nurses wearing white caps and long lines of patients receiving medications. Some of them were small and cozy and looked like somebody's summer home, full of patterned rugs and furniture and old books and magazines. We set up the videodisc wherever we could — in an office, a beauty shop, or wherever it was possible.

Once again, if not for the special circumstances afforded by my post-doctoral fellowship, it would not have been possible to carry out this research project. Out in the beautiful Missouri farmlands, hidden on quiet roads frequented by wandering farm animals, we found here and there a cluster of interested ex-psychiatric patients.

In our research study, we standardized the length of time that each viewer interacted with the videodisc. There were two ways in which we instructed them to interact with the disc. For their first and last trials, they received what we called the test instructions, in which they were encouraged to make whatever choices would keep Cathy as well as possible. On the in-between trials, they received what we called the practice instructions, which encouraged them to make any choice that they wanted in order to see what would happen.

Further preparation of the subjects with respect to exploring the undesirable paths on the disc might have enabled them to learn more. Several of the research participants, when asked to pick choices that they did not consider the most desirable in order to see the less desirable consequences, seemed unable to view these undesirable consequences with an experimental attitude. One subject, after doing well under the test instructions, picked some alternative paths on the practice instructions and appeared distressed at Cathy having to be readmitted. He seemed to want further time with the disc to comprehend these paths better. One or two subjects, after having viewed some of the less desirable sequences, chose for Cathy to return to the hospital on their last test trial. They felt, having viewed the less desirable endings on the practice trials, that she needed to be hospitalized.

14

Measuring Changes in Maladaptive Cognitions

In this chapter I discuss the nature of the maladaptive cognitions that we were measuring and why psychotic people have so many of these troublesome beliefs. I also discuss why working with the chronically mentally ill is difficult and takes so long, but why this work can be of great value.

Our technique of measuring the effect of the Cathy videodisc was, of course, a primary focus of our research efforts. I was faced with the task of measuring the effect of vicariously illustrating to the viewer a number of different adaptive behaviors, none of which was covered exhaustively. I designed the story to capture the attention of the patient, and I felt that this could be accomplished best by sticking to behaviors that could have plausibly occurred in the life of the main character during the course of the story. In other words, I gave precedence to the process of creating the disc rather than to the process of measuring the effect of the disc. I was concerned that, if I designed the disc to exhaustively cover one particular behavior that was conveniently measurable, the disc might not be interesting enough to be effective. I was, thus, committed to designing a way of measuring the viewer's learning from the Cathy story rather than writing the story to try to improve the viewer's performance on some previously existing psychological measure.

Having designed the disc in this way, I was able to measure the subjects' grasp of the concepts conveyed on the videodisc by creating a questionnaire. This was called the Wellness-Maintenance Questionnaire. I wrote true-false items, such as "Clumsy people should stay home,"

"Some people have all the answers," and "Healthy people expect each other to make some mistakes." There were also multiple choice questions having to do with problem situations similar to those encountered on the videodisc, such as someone planning to stand in line at a clinic.

We did a number of things to make the questionnaires easy to use. They were typed in large print because patients frequently misplace their eyeglasses. The vocabulary was simple so that educational level did not affect performance on the questionnaire. In general, the patients liked the questionnaires; one of our patients asked to keep his copy, stating that it was "worthy of study."

We indeed found that our experimental group made significantly greater gains in their Wellness-Maintenance scores than the control group (see Olevitch & Hagan, 1991). We also found that the Wellness-Maintenance scores of our schizophrenic subjects were significantly lower than those of a sample of hospital employees, indicating that the maladaptive cognitions that we measured occurred far more frequently in the schizophrenic sample.

These kinds of questionnaire items measure something very important for the rational emotive behavioral or cognitive therapist who is planning psychoeducational groups or developing psychoeducational materials. The psychosis of the patient is not directly amenable to therapy, but maladaptive cognitions, which hamper the patient in the management of his or her emotions and daily decision making, are amenable to therapy.

I do not regard the patient's endorsing the item "Clumsy people should stay home" as a sign or symptom of a problem such as irrationality, psychoticism, or impaired judgment. I regard the patient's agreement with this item as a cognitive behaviorist would regard a problem behavior. The belief is not a sign or symptom of an underlying problem — the belief itself is a problem. This belief will hamper the patient repeatedly as long as he or she believes it. In my view, this belief is amenable to direct intervention. Anything that will affect the patient's belief in this item — discussions, encouragement, modeling, practice, and so on — will affect the patient's functioning in a favorable direction.

Why are people who have suffered from a psychotic condition troubled by so many maladaptive cognitions? Possibly they begin with more irrational thoughts than nonpsychotic people have to cope with, but they may also have less experience in talking themselves out of these irrational thoughts. Where do the kinds of adaptive cognitions come from that enable individuals to talk themselves out of their own maladaptive cognitions? Strength in coping can be a natural endowment, and it can also be learned from imitating others, either on the basis of individual relationships or by membership in a larger community that shares ideas.

The cognitive deficits and idiosyncrasies of the psychosis-prone individual can be a handicap in maintaining the close communication with others that is needed to fully absorb and master a good set of coping beliefs, as well as some strategies for designing one's life in a manageable way. Moreover, the lives of psychosis-prone individuals are interrupted so many times by psychotic episodes that they are prevented from maintaining the connections and commitments that would help them exercise and refine their beliefs by putting them into action. They continuously have to start over to define their priorities and develop their relationships, skills, routines, and beliefs.

Awareness of these difficulties can actually give the therapist a more optimistic view of the potential value of an educational experience especially designed for teaching the psychotic individual how to talk himself out of maladaptive cognitions. Individuals who have not developed the kinds of beliefs that enable them to become resilient may be helped to do so. Ordinary people who could never have invented algebra or calculus on their own can nevertheless learn it from others; similarly, those who are not endowed with a natural cognitive facility or emotional resilience, and who haven't yet had a good opportunity to learn this from others, can learn it if they have sufficient exposure to it in special circumstances where cognitive-emotional maneuvers are shared and highlighted and where therapists have experience with different ways of thinking.

We did not conceptualize the cognitions measured by the Wellness-Maintenance Questionnaire as being permanent beliefs of the individual, but as being the kind of cognitions that change over time. When someone is fired from a job or locks himself out of his apartment, he walks around for a certain period of time thinking "I am stupid." Hopefully, he soon snaps out of this, either by arguing with himself or consoling himself in some way. What a clinician really needs to be able to see is whether the belief "I am stupid" is active or inactive at a certain time. Even the most chronic psychiatric patient has times when he does not believe that he is hopeless. The purpose of a measure such as this is to see how many maladaptive beliefs are currently active.

Given our view that even a few maladaptive cognitions can impair a person's functioning to some extent, we regarded our finding that the experimental group made greater gains than the control group as indicating that the two sessions our subjects spent with the videodisc were of some clinical significance. We might speculate that, in the future, an educational program including more interactive material over a longer period of time might be even more helpful.

A therapist who is designing cognitively-oriented groups for chronically mentally ill patients needs to have some sort of metaphor in mind for understanding why working to correct a multitude of maladaptive cognitions is hard and uncertain work and why it takes a long time. The nature of this metaphor will determine the therapist's pace and the therapist's feeling of accomplishment.

One such metaphor is computer programs. As anyone who has worked with computers knows, the entire output of a computer program can become complete nonsense because of a tiny typographical error in the input. It may be hard to find the error, but once it is found, it is not difficult to correct. Then, once the first problem is corrected, other problems appear that were there all along waiting to happen, but they remained undiscovered because of all the trouble caused by the first problem. With sufficient time, the bugs can be corrected, and the computer program begins to function. The amount of disturbance in the output does not necessarily mean that there is no solution.

Working with chronically mentally ill people is similar to this process. When a person experiences some clinical improvement and gains more confidence, all of a sudden she begins to focus on a myriad of practical problems that had been there all along but to which she had given no attention. Her driver's license has expired, she has no furniture, she needs new eyeglasses, she has no ongoing activities in which she is interested, and so on. It can be many months before she can actually begin to function independently. The patient is aware of all of this work that needs to be done to get her back into a functional life-style, and she finds it discouraging to think about, especially because she knows that she may have future relapses. An observer who was noting merely that she had made therapeutic improvement but was still not functioning might speculate that her initiative or judgment had been irreparably damaged by her psychotic disorder. Instead, the patient might be inwardly considering whether it was worth summoning up the energy to do all of this work, knowing that many social barriers awaited her. A therapist who expects these new problems can feel encouraged and see them as a sign of progress.

Another metaphor that helps me to focus on clearing up obstacles without expecting immediate results is to visualize a highly intelligent, well-motivated individual sitting in a wheelchair, unable to mount the steps into a university library. The installation of a ramp can change the entire course of this individual's development, but the effects would not be noticed right away. The person would have to wait a year before she could make the university application deadline, and she would have to build up the sense of commitment that it takes to go to school once the age of the usual college years is past. She would have to learn her way around the library before she could use it, and so on.

The therapist can gain a sense of purpose by realizing that certain maladaptive cognitions can be just as powerful as the absence of a ramp in blocking someone's development, even if the person had all of the other necessary traits and skills for whatever she was intending to do. Each time the patient's ability to use adaptive cognitions is strengthened, it is as if a new ramp is built, enabling the patient to go a little further with her planning process. From her new vantage point, she can perhaps comprehend a little more than she could before. Although she may still have many limitations, with more adaptive cognitions she can take her own limitations into account with increasing accuracy and gradually build a sounder foundation for her future life.

15

Computerized Interactive Media as Future Treatment and Research Tools

Computerized interactive media are feasible treatment tools for hospitals and mental health centers. They also have great potential for making cognitive interventions more repeatable and testable for research purposes.

Many researchers have concluded that it is difficult for clients to apply complex skills learned in social skills groups to ever-changing outside situations (Liberman, Mueser, Wallace, Jacobs, Eckman, & Massel, 1986) and that their learning may not last over long periods of time (Bellack & Mueser, 1993). Because interactive media can help us to repeat a treatment more cost-effectively, the fact that the treatment only helps for a short time becomes less of a problem. The duration of positive effects of treatment can be studied, and plans can be made accordingly. If the effect of a treatment only lasts a month, it can be repeated monthly. If an educational program only helps patients develop a certain behavior in a certain situation, a whole library of educational programs can be developed, each of which helps patients within a certain narrow area of behavior.

The development of this kind of software is only beginning, but innovators are already setting up centers where patients can use these materials (see Barsh & Jackson, 1996). The development of a greater variety of research-tested materials for use in these centers would be a worthwhile challenge to the psychologists and other mental health practitioners of this generation and the next.

Since completing the research project evaluating the Cathy videodisc, I have presented the Cathy disc to numerous audiences and shown it to patients under a variety of circumstances. I have become even more persuaded that using this new medium for the chronically mentally ill is feasible and likely to be productive in mental health centers and hospitals. I have shown the disc to patients in groups and individually (with and without their therapists) and in a patient library setting. The clinical staff at numerous facilities have been enthusiastic about the disc and the medium. Not only were they enthusiastic about using the disc, but they generally had a lot of good ideas about other discs that would be helpful. Many wanted to become involved in making such discs. I have mailed "Cathy" to different facilities, accompanied by only brief instructions about how to use it, and many different groups of people have succeeded in running the program. It is currently being used successfully in several patient library settings, along with other kinds of computer-aided instructional tools (Barsh & Jackson, 1996), and it is being set up for use in several other facilities as well.

The topic of expenses always comes up. During the last few years, most mental health centers and hospitals have acquired computers. The expense of setting up a videodisc system has consequently gone down because only the videodisc player must be added to the equipment already in place, and there are relatively inexpensive videodisc players available that are designed for educational applications (see Olevitch & Hagan, 1994, for more details about equipment).

Some people feel that the equipment necessary to set up instructional programs using interactive media is too expensive for a mental health center. Other people do not feel that this is the case; I have had administrators comment to me that equipment for showing the Cathy program could pay for itself because patient use could be billed as discharge planning. Also, given the high cost of hospital treatment, if routine use of the Cathy program even slightly shortened the stay of a few patients, this effect would add up to pay for the cost of the equipment.

Nevertheless, I am actually uncomfortable with any argument that these programs will pay for themselves because I believe that, even if they were more expensive and did not pay for themselves, they would still be worthwhile because they help patients to achieve their goals.

It has always been hard to justify psychotherapeutic approaches for severe mental illness; there is still not enough of a consensus that a psychological approach to the seriously mentally ill has any validity. It is very hard to obtain funding for anything that isn't completely tangible. Computerized interactive media, however, have the potential to make psychological interventions more tangible, repeatable, and testable, so that consistent positive effects may at last be made visible even to the most skeptical.

IV

GROUP WORKSHOPS IN RESIDENTIAL CARE SETTINGS

This section contains questions and demonstrations used and actual reactions of groups in a series of workshops given for mentally ill clients living in residential community settings.

16

"Deeper" Cognitive
Interventions

We have been talking at a workshop about reality and how the human senses are limited. I have pointed out that scientists are very careful to gather different kinds of evidence about reality so they can check one form of evidence against another. The topic of planets comes up. I ask, "How many planets are there?" I get a few different answers, "eight," "nine." One woman says "26." Later, after the workshop, she approaches me. "I had forgotten about the planets," she says, looking surprised and pleased. "It's a good thing you came." Later on, her case manager said that she had greatly improved since the workshop.

Using a rational emotive behavioral or cognitive approach toward understanding psychotic people altered more than just my treatment sessions with patients. These theories deepened my understanding of the nature of the problems faced by chronically mentally ill individuals. I also realized that patients often had the ability to comprehend these problems in greater detail than is usually offered in psychoeducational groups. I wanted to go beyond the content that I had been able to express using dramatized video and to develop group workshops that addressed some of these deeper concerns.

I had an opportunity to offer some longer workshops to ex-patients in residential care settings in the community. I would be traveling to remote locations alone and without video equipment. Because the residents would be living in these settings for a while, and because they would not have the same level of acute distress as hospital patients, this was an opportunity to develop my thinking on these deeper topics that might take more sessions to discuss in detail. At different settings, I ran workshops that ranged from 2 to 48 sessions.

Taking a cognitive view of human behavior does not mean focusing only on irrational statements, it means taking the context in which the patient generated these statements seriously. When a person has a problem and cannot arrive at a productive view of the problem, he becomes more vulnerable to irrational explanations, such as "I am a failure."

Where does a person's supply of productive explanations come from? Although each person only has limited access to information and limited life experiences, it appears that each person within his own mind seeks to explain in some fashion the totality of human experience in considerable detail. People develop quite an extensive set of ideas about where they fit into the totality of human experience and where they stand in comparison to others on varying dimensions. In an effort to predict and control reality and make good decisions, each individual accumulates hypotheses and theories of varying complexity and accuracy.

Given the difficulty of generating creative theories to explain reality, most people do not generate these theories entirely on their own; instead, they borrow extensively from a multitude of different sources. They may begin by adopting views similar to their parents and family, but ordinarily they graft onto these initial views other views that they adopt from teachers, friends, acquaintances, books, television, advertisements, movies, various subcultures, and the culture at large, as well as some of their own creative additions.

A person's explanatory and decision-making system is thus very complicated and bears the imprint of his prior social and intellectual life.

Although people work on and improve their explanatory system in their free time, almost as a sort of hobby, for practical purposes a person does not need to turn to his own unique explanatory system very often. Under normal circumstances cognitive activity revolves around some set of attachments and goals that are taken for granted, a set of expected problems in maintaining these attachments and achieving these goals, and some expected sources of help.

When a person has a set of attachments and commitments that occupy him on a daily basis they have an organizing effect upon the person's cognitive activity. Worries about man's inhumanity to man and why the world is the way it is constitute a sort of background noise. Superimposed over this background noise are practical concerns with current deadlines: how to get to work if the car doesn't start, what to do about an aging household appliance, what to eat for supper, and so on.

Another reason why the explanatory systems of people leading smoothly running lives do not come up very often is that they have gravitated, over the years, to people with compatible explanatory concepts and values, so that much is taken for granted and needs no attention or articulation.

Psychotic or chronically mentally ill people usually lack the comfortable attachments and goals that characterize the person with the smoothly running life. During the course of their illness, they may have become alienated from family and friends and occupationally displaced, their education may have been interrupted, and they may have fallen into socioeconomic conditions different from those to which they were accustomed. They must make increased demands upon their explanatory system just when it has been repeatedly jarred. Feeling ill at ease in their situation and their perspectives, the mentally ill often develop an affinity for profound or highly general topics for which ordinary busy people don't have time. A therapist wishing to conduct a discussion group can make use of this affinity. After a person has remained in bed every day for a while, a topic has to sound important to justify getting out of bed to talk about it. Someone who has spent the last few years in a state of general retreat can enter into a general discussion on human nature or a cosmic philosophical topic a lot more easily than he can make small talk because small talk requires that you keep up with what is occurring currently. A broad, philosophical general topic, however, puts everyone on an equal footing.

It is very rewarding in a discussion group when some quiet soul who doesn't ordinarily attend groups speaks up and says something like "I try to make meaning in everything I say and do," and you know that you have guided a group discussion in such a way that this comment fits in and is perceived by the other group members as a contribution.

To summarize, I had two goals in these workshops. First, I used the intense focus of many mentally ill people upon their personal explanatory systems as a way of engaging their participation. Second, I offered explanatory concepts that might be valuable additions to those that they already had. I took my own most valuable explanatory concepts — ideas from the psychological literature that I had found to be the most applicable to patients — and explained these to the groups.

I enjoyed these workshops. I felt, more so than at any other time, that I was able to facilitate communication between group members that was not superficial. I think that the workshops helped the participants to feel understood.

I am including here some notes on a series of topics in the hope that they will enable the reader to capture and re-create the mood of these kinds of workshops. The answers given after each question are a compilation of answers given or developed by different groups.

The mechanics of the workshops were fairly simple. I always brought a portable easel with a large pad. I always printed out the title of the workshop on the first page and displayed it prominently. I also wrote out, in advance, definitions, statements, and lists of concepts that I was going to use, as well as simple drawings to use as the workshop proceeded. I left blank pages in between for recording group responses. I always tried to come up with stories or anecdotes that were pertinent.

Although I sometimes used handouts, I believe that showing the outline on a pad is preferable to distributing handouts during the discussion. The attention of easily distracted participants can be synchronized with the pad because the leader has more control over the timing of when they read it. The pad is preferable to a blackboard because it can be prepared in advance. I often brought paper or small notebooks and pencils in case anybody wanted to take notes.

I did the printing and drawing by hand and used large print and bright colors. I did not try to save these pages for subsequent workshops but wrote and drew on them during the workshop to emphasize or expand upon various points. After the workshop, I could use these notes to reorganize the material for the next time I did the same topic with a different group.

I posted my topics in advance on the bulletin boards in the residential homes. Nevertheless, I arrived an hour early and walked around with a clipboard with the workshop title and approached residents individually to encourage attendance.

When I gave a long series of workshops, I gave out fancy attendance and award certificates to the residents at the final session. I heard from the staff that residents were very pleased with these.

17

Workshop:
How Many Needs Do We Really Have?

I asked: *How many needs do people have?* I made this a multiple choice question, giving the group answers, such as 5, 10, 15, 20, or 25 or more. I then went around the group getting responses. The responses varied widely.

I asked: *Why is "how many needs?" possibly a confusing question?* They responded that some things are needed for life and some things are needed for a happy life.

I then asked: *Do people always know what they need?* The group agreed that no, sometimes they neglect things they really need and sometimes people think they need more than they do. I then asked for examples, such as the fact that alcoholics often don't eat well.

I asked: *How do people feel if they think they need more than they do?* They suggested these people feel frustrated, miserable, scared, anxious, angry, and frantic.

Then I asked: *What things are essential for life?* The list decided on was food, shelter, clothes, air, and medical care.

Finally, I asked: *What things are essential for happiness?* The group's responses included your own phone, money, transportation, voting, freedom of speech, tools, choices, entertainment, companionship, literacy, security, cleanliness, health information, materials, appliances, machines, possessions, justice system, order, sleep, babies, love, friendship, sex, mercy, prayers, self-esteem, self-confidence, family, sense of meaning, cigarettes, someone to talk to, television, travel, comfort, not to be criticized, and attention.

If you discuss, in general, how people feel when they think they need more than they really need before you get to the point of making the lists of needs, then people are already warmed up to the idea that they will be better off if they can eliminate items from their list of needs rather than adding items. Having prepared the group by talking ahead of time about how people often think they need more than they actually do, the group members don't feel embarrassed about suggesting needs that the others don't agree are needs.

I remember vividly one workshop held in a small residential facility in the countryside where the group actually applauded at the end.

There were several lively exchanges during the workshop, one based upon a discussion of our need for money, another upon a discussion of our need for love. Some groups members had listed these as necessary for life.

When I challenged the group by questioning, "do we really need money?" I got an immediate response.

"Of course," a great majority of the group agreed, "we would die without money. You need money to eat."

I was surprised that so many of the group believed this, particularly because many of them had been through periods when they were without income.

I agreed, of course, that we need food to live, but not that we need money. It took a bit of discussion before the group members gradually pieced together an account of the actual relationship between money and eating in our society. It is highly desirable to have your own money so that you can go to the store and buy food, but if, for some reason, this isn't possible, there are often people who will help you and feed you, such as your family and friends. Many charities exist that help people get food. Many churches would help a member or even possibly a stranger in need. There are also government programs that provide food stamps and shelters that provide some meals.

A person without money might feel embarrassed to ask for help, but it is better to feel embarrassed than to starve. If a person is willing to seek help when he doesn't have money, his chances of finding food are good, because there are many people in our society who are willing to make sure that poor people don't starve, especially when they are disabled.

I explained that often, you hear people say that "you have to work to eat," but sometimes people say things like this just to encourage themselves and others to work hard so that they don't have to ask others for help. They don't really mean that they would die if they ran out of money.

After a while the group had to admit that, instead of saying we need money to live, it would be more accurate to say that having money was the most convenient way to live. Life without money might be inconvenient, and there might be a lot of embarrassment involved in having to ask for help frequently, but it is certainly possible in our society to survive physically without an income, especially if you are disabled.

The exchange about needing love to live was equally lively. I argued that many people go through periods when they are not in any kind of loving relationship, even with family. People may come from a small family and family members may have died, have been victims of war, or be estranged for various reasons. Yet people survive and possibly even enjoy some happiness in doing so. I stuck to this position despite the eloquence of group members about how everyone needs love. Finally I conceded only that the hope of love in the future may be critical.

The applause at the end of the workshop surprised me, and I interpret it as agreement with the position I was taking. It must be a relief to people who may feel unloved that this is not a desperate need and is something to hope for rather than something that one cannot do without.

18

Workshop:
Perception

I asked: *Are people who are not mentally ill always right about what they see, hear, feel, touch, and so on?* If the group did not arrive at the correct answer, I explained that the senses of the normal human being are far from perfect. I explained further that if the senses were perfect, that would mean that what was seen, heard, and so on, would perfectly match what was in the outside world. Senses are only imperfect tools that help us to figure out what is in the outside world.

At this point I gave examples of illusions. I used two demonstrations. One was a large red circle on a poster. The group looked at it for 20 seconds. Then I put up a blank piece of paper. They all saw a green circle that wasn't really there, that is, the after-image from fixating the red circle.

A second demonstration that I used was always especially successful. If you can find something like this, it is well worth the trouble, because of the fun the group has with it. I have a gadget (the same device that was described earlier in this book in Part I, Chapter 4, "Hallucinations") that consists of a mirror-lined bowl with a space in the middle of the lid. When a penny is placed in the bottom of the bowl, it creates an illusion. When looked at from a slight distance, it appears that the penny is sitting in the space in the middle of the lid, but when you try to touch what you think is a penny, it simply isn't there. The gadget creates what is called a virtual image, and it startles and amuses everybody.

I had people line up and try to touch the penny. They each laughed when they felt nothingness instead of the penny they expected.

I warned them ahead of time that it wasn't really there, but they should try to touch it anyway so that they could see that not everything we see is really there. Even knowing this in advance, they still felt startled when they couldn't feel the penny.

Other possible examples that can be used are: showing other illusions, pointing out that dogs can smell more than people can and birds can see more, and discussing how illnesses or drugs can create sensory impairments or strange sensations.

I asked: *If our senses are so imperfect, how can we tell what is really in the outside world and what is not?* I guided the group until they arrived at the conclusion that sometimes we can't! There are many things that we would like to know that scientists have been unable to find out. When we are interested in finding out more about something, we use certain ways of checking whether our senses are correct, and we also use other tools to gather information. But, of course, we are not always successful. There are still many things that we do not understand.

I asked: *What are some of the ways that we check the information that we get from our senses?* Groups were able to develop the idea that we check one sense against another, check one person's perception against another, and keep records and check something repeatedly over time.

I asked: *If our senses are only one set of tools we use to find out about reality, what are some of the other tools?* The groups listed two kinds of tools we use:

devices — eyeglasses, microscopes, cameras, telescopes, seismographs, contact lenses, magnifying glasses, x-rays, seeing eye dogs, electrocardiograms, calculators, computers, and so on,

our intelligence — scientists design experiments to figure things out; we use our intelligence to figure out the meaning of what we see.

I emphasized throughout that these tools are also imperfect — sometimes when we use reasoning to figure out the significance of what we see, we make mistakes in our reasoning. It is good to remember that we are never totally sure about what is really in the outside world and that, in order to understand reality as well as we can, we need to do a lot of checking. It's good to be humble about what we think. Everybody makes mistakes.

I asked: *If normal human senses aren't perfect, why are people so upset about someone hearing voices or seeing things that aren't there?*

The material in this workshop seems to prepare group members to talk about the experience of being psychotic. By the time I got to the final question about why it bothers people that some people hear voices that aren't there, I got a wide variety of interesting individual reactions.

19

Workshop:
After a Mental Illness

RECOVERING FROM THE SHOCK

I explained that *when something bad happens, people often feel sad or angry. They also feel puzzled and ask themselves a lot of big questions.*

I showed a stick figure whose head was surrounded by question marks. I pointed out that his head was so full of questions that he could hardly "fit in" anything else.

I asked: *Do you know what I mean by the kinds of big questions that people ask themselves when something bad happens?*

Groups responded to this question by giving heart-rending examples of their feelings about their mental illness and psychiatric hospitalization.

What did I do wrong?
Who is to blame?
Will it happen again?
Will I be able to cope?
Why me?
Why?
Why can't they help me more?

What causes it?

Why don't people understand?

I explained that *how people answer these big questions influences their feelings.* I began to discuss some examples while making a chart with three columns, one called "situation" or "event" for a very brief description of the situation, one headed by a sad face to list thoughts about the event that might lead people to feel bad, and one headed by a happy face to list the kinds of thoughts about the same event that might make people feel better.

For example, one man talked about how he felt at family gatherings. He felt like he "didn't fit in." He described how one relative had a pacemaker and another was very old. He concluded, "I don't belong here." I discussed how thinking "I don't belong here" gives a person sort of a spooky feeling, as if he were not part of the real world. I gave an example of an old scary T.V. program called the Twilight Zone, where a woman who looked just like the main character stole her bus ticket and was going to continue with the woman's life. The main character was left stranded in the bus terminal with no life to go back to. I suggested that if instead of thinking "I don't belong here" he were to think "I'm bored" he would feel differently. The whole group laughed when they heard "I'm bored" as another response to the same situation. They could see that the thought "I'm bored" didn't lead to feelings that were so hard to deal with. The thought "I'm bored" made the problem seem very temporary and something that could be dealt with by looking for more meaningful connections and activities.

Emphasize alternate explanations that reduce self-blame and anger at others and increase acceptance of not knowing exactly why the problems occurred.

FINDING YOUR WAY AGAIN

I drew a cartoon picture of a stick figure sitting on the road as if it had fallen out of a moving bus. The bus moves on and it is left there on the road. I related this illustration to the idea of falling behind because of an episode of mental illness. The image of the figure sitting on the road while the bus continues without it can be used as a metaphor for experiences, such as dropping out of school in the middle of the semester or when a temporary illness displaces the individual in such a way that it becomes difficult to continue with his or her previous plans. This topic stimulates group members to relate a lot of important experiences shared by the chronically mentally ill having to do with falling behind their peers. One group member told of having to return to high school at the age of 28. One talked about realizing that all of his friends were married and had families.

Getting started again involves a lot of hard work redoing things that have been done before, for example, getting a driver's license and making decisions about where to live and what to do. Tasks involved in this stage include:

rebuilding "image" and regaining the trust of others,

finding new goals — being willing to commit oneself to goals that are different from what one wanted before, and

finding a new pace that suits how one feels.

The groups became involved in commenting on each of these.

ADJUSTING TO PSYCHIATRIC SYMPTOMS

The following could be used as a handout and the group can discuss each item:

Having symptoms can be a little easier if you:

1. Don't think less of yourself
2. Don't give up
3. Don't blame yourself
4. Don't blame others
5. Try not to be afraid
6. Accept not knowing exactly why this happened to you

20

Workshop:
Everybody's Different

I introduced this workshop by stating: Today we're going to talk about differences in personality. Many people have invented ways of looking at how people are different from one another. A lot of these ways of looking at differences are judgmental — for example, you might describe people as either mature or immature. We are going to talk about differences in personality as described by someone named Isabel Briggs Myers. She believed that people are different from each other but that one type of person is not better than another type of person.

I asked: *What are the disadvantages of people being different from one another?* The groups gave varied answers, such as

lack of understanding,
misunderstanding,
friction,
put-downs,
efforts to change one another,
arguments,
fights,
wars,
working at cross-purposes, and
disappointment.

I asked: *What are the advantages of people being different?* The groups gave two main advantages: everything gets done and it makes life interesting.

I asked: *What if we aren't aware of differences that exist?* The groups answered that we might keep wondering why we're not like others, we might keep wondering why others aren't like us, or we might keep expecting the wrong things from the wrong people.

I introduced this part of the workshop by saying: We are going to talk about some individual differences following this format. I'll put some ways in which people are different on the board, for example,

Talks a lot   Concise

Then we'll talk about the ways in which people with these characteristics see each other. For each pair of characteristics, we'll talk about the possible negative ways that they might see each other if they don't understand their differences in personality. We'll also discuss the possible positive ways that they could see each other if they keep their personality differences in mind.

In my workshops, I would draw an arrow arching from "talks a lot" to "concise" and ask, "When they don't understand each other, how might somebody who talks a lot feel about somebody who likes to talk very briefly?" A group member might say, "The person feels rejected, like the other person doesn't want to talk to him because he doesn't like him." I would write "feel rejected" along the arrow. Then I would draw another arrow and ask, "When two people don't understand each other, how might somebody who likes to be concise feel about somebody who likes to talk a lot?" A group member might say, "The person feels like the person who talks a lot is pushy and takes up a lot of his time and won't let him go." I would write "pushy" along the arrow that I had drawn.

I would explain that the person who likes to talk a lot probably doesn't always understand that some people like to be concise because it is part of their personalities. Once the person who likes to talk a lot realizes this, then he doesn't expect the concise person to talk a lot, and he doesn't feel rejected. The concise person can realize that the person who enjoys talking a lot isn't being inconsiderate and tying up the concise person's time. He is just communicating the way he usually does.

Then I would draw another arch with an arrow and ask, "Once the concise person understands that the other person enjoys talking a lot, can he see something positive about the person who talks a lot?"

A group member related that she was usually very concise and had a hard time making conversation at dinners or parties. She really enjoyed sitting next to someone who talked a lot at a social gathering. I wrote "fun at a party" along the arrow.

I drew one final arrow and asked, "When the person who talks a lot understands the concise person better, what can he see about him that is positive?"

The group members agreed that when you need to find information about something, it was wonderful to find someone who could explain it to you concisely without adding too many extra details. Also, it is a lot easier to get to talk to a concise person, because you don't have to wait so long before they are available.

Another difference to discuss involves people who like to talk about

"What if" and "maybe"   Real people and things

The people who like to talk about "what if" feel at times that the others are narrow-minded, while the people who prefer real things feel that the others are impractical. People who prefer real things sometimes feel that those concerned with "what if" are too nervous. The people who like to talk about "what if" can get good day-to-day practical advice from those who prefer sticking to current reality. The people who prefer sticking to current reality can sometimes get important warning signals from those who concern themselves with hypothetical situations about problems that might arise in the future.

Another discussion topic involves people who like to be

Well-organized   Spontaneous

Spontaneous people sometimes feel that well-organized people are missing out on a lot, while well-organized people sometimes feel that spontaneous people are drifters. Well-organized people often find that spontaneous people are fun to be around, and spontaneous people often find that well-organized people can contribute a lot toward making things safer and more secure.

Another example is people who prefer to focus on

Facts and logic   Feelings

People who prefer to focus on facts and logic sometimes see people who focus on feelings as irrational or biased, while people who prefer to focus on feelings sometimes see people who focus on logic as cold. People who prefer to focus on feelings sometimes appreciate some critical feedback from a more logic-oriented person when they are trying to make a balanced decision, and people who focus on logic sometimes appreciate some feedback from a more emotion-based person when they are trying to decide what their priorities should be.

A final example is people who prefer

Peace and quiet   Lots of people and excitement

Sometimes people who prefer having a lot of people around think that those who prefer peace and quiet are nervous, while people who prefer peace and quiet may feel intimidated by those who like to have a lot of people around. People who prefer to have a lot of people around sometimes turn to those who like peace and quiet for some good ideas, and people who prefer peace and quiet sometimes turn to those who prefer having a lot of people around when they need to make some important contacts for getting something done.

This topic of individual differences generates a lot of discussion and can be used for two or three sessions. I thought it was more important to focus on misunderstandings generated by opposite characteristics, taken one at a time, than to convey to the group didactic material about the personality types described by Isabel Briggs Myers, which are more complex constellations of characteristics. If a group leader would like to get more of a feeling for this subject, he or she can read *Gifts Differing* (Briggs Myers & Myers, 1980).

21

Workshop:
Ideas Are Hard to Change

I began this workshop by stating: Today we're going to talk about what goes on inside the mind. There are some people who are known as famous thinkers who have written some very thick books that you can find in the library. But it isn't only famous thinkers who have a lot of thoughts and knowledge. Ordinary people also have a lot of thoughts and knowledge. Their thoughts and knowledge can also be very organized.

In my workshop, I drew an illustration consisting of a square with a double line around it in which I wrote "SURE." Around this square, I drew another square in which I wrote "UNSURE." Around the outer square I put a lot of question marks.

Using this illustration, I began a discussion of how there are certain things that we feel absolutely sure of that nothing could make us doubt, other things that we have absolutely no knowledge of, and some things in between. For these in-between things, we may have a little knowledge but we're not sure of it, or we might think we know something and be mistaken.

I pointed out how people differ in how much they think they are sure of. Some people won't believe anything until they see a lot of proof, and some people will pass on beliefs that they have only heard once.

The group gave examples of some things they were sure of, totally ignorant of, or unsure of and some people who were either skeptical or easily accepting of beliefs.

I asked: *What do beliefs consist of?* They consist, first of all, of some sort of list of what you believe exists. I made a sample list that included cats, dogs, unicorns, and "people who never do anything right."

The group agreed that the last two items didn't really exist. In one group, a member said she thought unicorns really existed. That gave us an opportunity to talk about what a funny feeling it is when you think something is true and you find out it isn't. The group could see that even the lists of items that you have in mind as existing can be controversial.

People may have in their minds a list of statements, some of which they believe to be true and some of which they believe to be false. Examples of statements might be:

All cats are animals.

All dogs are animals.

All unicorns are animals.

I am a cat.

I am a dog.

The group could see that if the existence of an item, such as a unicorn, is in question, it is difficult to say whether any of the statements about unicorns are true or false. If there are really dogs and cats, then it is easy to see that it is false that a person is a dog or a cat. But when someone has a concept like "a failure," if there is really no such thing as a failure, then the person's statements about under what conditions she becomes a failure are not exactly true or false but confusing and nonsensical.

I introduced the idea that statements in the mind are often organized into arguments, which are strings of statements that are connected. I drew an illustration that looked like a pile of bricks. All the bottom bricks were labelled "premise," and the top one was labelled "conclusion."

I then gave a classic example of an argument, explaining that it is a connected group of statements in which some of the statements are premises and some of the statements are conclusions that follow from the premises.

All men are mortal.

Socrates is a man.

Socrates is mortal.

I gave some examples of emotional reasoning, where it could be seen that some of the premises and the conclusions were questionable.

There are some people who never do anything right.

I make a lot of mistakes.

I must be one of those people who never does anything right.

The group easily identified the wrong reasoning in these kinds of arguments.

A few more illustrations were used to stimulate discussion about how ideas sometimes don't change because the person who has them doesn't challenge them.

I drew an illustration of a face with a little cartoon cloud with the word "ideas" in it. Outside of the face, I wrote the word "reality," with quotation marks. I pointed out that our conception of reality comes from what we see and how we interpret what we see.

An example of seeing someone with a sad look on her face gets the following possible interpretations from the group:

She doesn't like me.

She is a sad person.

Something sad must have just happened.

Life is miserable.

The group can discuss how the person who believes that "life is miserable" uses this to explain everything she sees and doesn't consider whether this is really true.

Another illustration of two faces, one happy and one sad, can be used to point out that the person who believes life is miserable goes around frowning at everyone and so has more negative experiences than others. This keeps the person from changing his belief.

Group reactions to this topic were a real surprise to me. I included the topic because I thought it was important, but I was afraid it would be rather dry. Their enthusiasm about this topic was greater than I expected. Because the topic was tightly organized and didn't lead off in too many directions, the group members enjoyed understanding the same thing at the same time. Therapists who would like to read a discussion of belief systems can see Abelson (1973).

22

Workshop:
What Is a Social Network and
Where Can I Find Mine?

I began with the following definition: *Social network — A set of different people that you can turn to for different things.*

I drew diagrams for two social networks, one very small and one very large. The small network consisted of two circles, joined by a large number of lines. I explained that it represents the smallest possible social network; it consists of an immigrant who doesn't speak English and his brother-in-law, who brought him to America and who is his boss. The many lines represent the different kinds of connections that he has to his brother-in-law.

"Who does he turn to when he needs to go somewhere?" I ask.

"To his brother-in-law," answers the group.

"Who does he turn to for help in filling out his taxes?"

"To his brother-in-law," the group answers.

"Who does he turn to when he just feels like talking to somebody?"

"To his brother-in-law," the group answers.

The second diagram, I explained, represents a very large social network. It is the social network of a college professor. The diagram consists of one circle in the middle, representing the professor, and a multitude of lines going out in every direction connecting with a multitude of other circles. I explained how the professor knows a large number of people who are each experts in a different area, and, whenever someone asks him a question, he can tell the person who she might go to who would know something about the question.

I asked: *How does a network get to be the way it is?* This answer usually did not emerge from the group. I provided the answer to this question because it gave the group the background for answering the questions that followed.

I stated that social networks evolve through a constant process of change, including growth, destruction, restoration, and maintenance.

I then asked: *What are the things that make social networks grow?* The groups may answer:

interests, hobbies,

common problems,

staying in the same place for a while,

chance encounters,

employment,

marriage,

making friends,

friends of friends,

having children,

having pets,

talking to neighbors or acquaintances,

organizations, and

getting involved in causes.

I asked: *What are the processes that reduce networks?* Groups answered:

neglect,

moves,

deaths,

divorces,

arguments, and

mental illness.

I then asked: *What are the processes that restore and maintain networks?* Answers included:

calling or writing letters,

starting over,

apologizing,

attending reunions,

making up, and

pursuing new interests and hobbies.

Throughout this session, group members can share stories about how their networks grew and how they shrank. Hearing stories from each other illustrates just how these processes work, such as how the death of one person can make you lose not just that person but a whole network of others that you knew through that person. Sometimes group members are able to share the feelings of embarrassment and envy that may cause them to procrastinate about getting in touch with people. Sometimes they share how they were able to have a feeling of belonging in some organization. By hearing each other, it becomes apparent that the feeling of belonging can be achieved in a number of different ways.

Helping patients to restore their "natural" social network is probably the most therapeutic thing a therapist can do. I once spent some time with a patient trying to locate her aunt. All the patient could remember was the restaurant chain and the neighborhood where the aunt worked. We called a few restaurants until we located her, and she began visiting the patient. I have rarely seen a client benefit so much from a single session.

Patients know that we are getting paid to see them and help them, so, in a way, what we do for them doesn't count. However, when they are able to restore a friendship or a helping relationship with a friend or relative or build a new relationship, this soothes their feeling of being unloved in a way that psychotherapy or a therapeutic milieu never can.

Because of their unusual way of expressing themselves, their unusual life situation, and their vulnerability to future episodes of mental illness, mentally ill people have a smaller choice of possible friends. They must choose someone who understands them and is willing to take the responsibility of having a friend with greater than average vulnerability. For all these reasons, they must endure more rejections than the ordinary person. If they understand this, they become more capable of persevering to seek the support they want.

There are several misconceptions in our oral tradition about seriously mentally ill people. Because of the stereotype, many people believe that patients with a serious mental illness are not capable of friendships and do not want them. This is not true. Mental illness strikes people of many different personality types; many mentally ill people are friendly individuals who like to become acquainted with large numbers of people. Some of them like to get to know only a few people but know them very well. The reasons for the shrinkage of each patient's social network are different. Even patients who seem withdrawn often still have relatives or friends who call or visit them or at least somebody that the patient still thinks about and with whom they could possibly get in touch.

Another somewhat opposite misconception about the mentally ill is the belief that they are dependent, whereas healthy people are independent. Cooperation and interdependence are very much a part of a healthy lifestyle. A person who accepts a degree of dependence upon others can achieve more than could be achieved alone.

The sad paradox is that, even though some mentally ill people seek more support than the average person, they often find less, even when the professional help they get is taken into account.

Because of their cognitive handicaps and symptoms, people who are prone to mental illness accumulate more problems than the average person. Moreover, they are less able to articulate these problems clearly and specifically. They may also feel so embarrassed about needing help that they wait until the problem is worse before asking for assistance. For all these reasons, when they finally reveal the extent of their difficulties, others may feel overwhelmed.

If mentally ill people can be unashamed to seek assistance with various matters and keep up with their everyday problems by asking questions and seeking assistance, then their problems will have less of a tendency to accumulate to the point of being overwhelming. The mentally ill person who realizes that the healthy person also seeks help from others can be persuaded to think about finding a whole network of people to relate to instead of finding one special other who will help him with everything.

I once treated a very intelligent woman who had suffered from severe psychotic symptoms over a period of many years. When she became distressed about a situation at home, her distress would take the form of psychiatric symptoms, and she would want psychiatric help. We discussed very explicitly the subject of different kinds of help. When you want help with a pipe, you call a plumber; when you want help with a car, you take it to a mechanic. This part was, of course, easy for her to grasp. Then we discussed situations where she wanted other kinds of help, for example, when she just felt like talking. She had a very large extended family, and she was able to think of several relatives that she could call just to talk. These were relatives that she had not been speaking to very much in the recent past, but for whom she had some affection. Over a period of time, she began telephone relationships with several people that she enjoyed talking to, and this was very helpful to her.

23

Workshop:
Self-Confidence

I asked: *How can you tell if someone is self-confident?*

The group answered: they don't hesitate, things seem easier, they are positive, more productive, and likeable. The group painted a sort of magical picture of the lucky creature called a "self-confident person." This person glided through difficulties easily, floated above doubts, and was always happy, well-liked, and productive.

I asked: *What is a self-confident person confident about?* The group answered that this person knew she could get things done. That gave me the opportunity to begin to challenge their conception of self-confidence, take it out of an unreachable magic realm, and make it realistically accessible.

I asked: *What if people don't achieve what they set out to? What if they are trying something that they know they might not be able to do, even with all their skills and even with help? Are there certain skills or talents — knowledge in a certain area, beauty, strength, athletic ability — that guarantee success in a particular endeavor?* Questions like these in a discussion with the group can begin to convey a different concept of confidence that is harder to grasp but easier to achieve. Confidence is not based upon any particular learned skill or any particular achievement but, rather, upon a commitment to keep on moving in a purposeful direction, even if the actual goals themselves have to be changed at times.

The confident person isn't saying to himself, "I can do it." He is saying, instead,

I would like to do this, but maybe I won't be able to.

I'll try my best by deciding what's most important and focusing on that, getting more information and help if I run into problems, and accepting my own limitations ahead of time so I can plan realistically.

I drew one of those cartoon figures walking confidently over the edge of a cliff without noticing. I explained that in the typical cartoon, this character keeps walking in the air until finally it looks down and notices that it is suspended. Only then does it become frightened and fall.

Discussion of the illustration can be used to make the point that the confident person isn't worried about being deflated because he is not inflated in the first place. He accepts that life is complicated and that achieving goals is a challenge.

24

Workshop:
It's a Crazy World

In general, as part of my preparation for each workshop, I posted the topic ahead of time on a bulletin board, if available. I also arrived about an hour early for the workshop, carrying a clipboard with the title of the workshop written in large print. I walked around and approached potential attendees to tell them about the workshop.

For this particular workshop, I believe that the mere reading of the title may be therapeutic. I never saw so many pleased smiles on the faces of the seriously mentally ill as I did the day I walked around with the clipboard with the title, "It's a Crazy World."

I asked: *Is it a crazy world?* I had the group take a vote. No one ever voted no. The answer was always unanimously yes.

I asked: *What are some examples of the world being crazy?* Answers from groups included:

people forget about important things;

there's a lot to worry about;

violence, crime;

disasters;

drugs;

habits;

lack of direction; and

styles.

I drew a picture of a stick figure facing a mountain peak in front of which a strange bird is walking around in circles. I put a big question mark next to the figure to indicate his puzzlement at the bird's strange behavior.

I asked: *How do you think he feels about not understanding the bird's behavior and about the fact that the bird's behavior seems crazy to him?* The group suggested he was amused and wondering.

I drew a picture of the same puzzled stick figure standing next to a small row of extraterrestrials, that is, some stick figures with upside down faces, little antennae, and upside down arms.

I asked: *How does he feel?* The group responded that he was amazed and curious.

I drew the same puzzled stick figure again. This time he was wearing a blue shirt and contemplating a row of other similar stick figures wearing green shirts. I explained that this indicates when the majority of people follow a certain convention that doesn't make sense to someone. I gave an example about a patient I once had who had a certain work skill but had never attended a training program and had no certification in this skill. To him, having to have certification in order to get a job seemed as incomprehensible as everyone wearing a green shirt.

I asked: *How does he feel?* The group decided he felt rejected and angry. "It doesn't make sense," one patient stated. "Why does everyone have to wear a green shirt?"

I discuss how, when I first learned that mentally ill people didn't accept reality, I didn't know what that meant. I pictured in my mind someone thinking that a triangle had five sides instead of three. To my surprise, I learned that what is usually meant by this is that there are some unpleasant things about human nature and culture that they do not wish to accept.

The stick figure didn't feel angry at the bird or at the extraterrestrials because he didn't think they should think just like him. He accepted their differences without any problem.

Improvement in accepting reality can come about by learning to view other people the same way that the stick figure viewed the bird and the extraterrestrials. If someone takes the attitude that other people's behavior doesn't necessarily have to make sense at any given moment, then he feels less shocked and angry. Feeling less angry at the world leads to feeling less blocked, less preoccupied, and less rejected.

I asked: *What could be the advantages of seeing the world as a crazy place?* When you have fewer specific expectations, you can feel less angry about the bad surprises and be more alert for surprisingly good things that you hadn't expected.

Seeing the world as incomprehensible can lead to enhanced opportunities and deeper understanding.

If you assume everyone values things just the way you do, you might be pessimistic about getting what you want. But if you understand that "one man's trash is another man's treasure," you might be open to seeing that there are desirable objects, desirable opportunities, and desirable friends available because not everyone is looking for what would please you.

To see the world as incomprehensible also helps you to open your mind to greater friendships for two reasons.

1. If you don't feel you must understand everything right away, you become more interested in hearing stories that other people tell.
2. When you're more aware of all that you don't understand, you begin to ask better questions and get to know people better.

25

Workshop:
Wondering Why? Why? Why?

I asked: *Is curiosity a strong feeling?* The group agreed that curiosity is surprisingly strong and motivates a lot of human behavior.

I asked: *How do scientists find out why something occurs?* Several possibilities are:

reading,

studying,

thinking,

performing experiments, and

using the scientific method.

I explained that even in science it is often hard to find out why things occur. When something is important to us, we often collect a lot of information about it, but certain problems can come up when we try to understand the information. Here is an example of a possible type of error that scientists have to watch out for.

Suppose a scientist collected this data (write the following on a blackboard or a flip pad.) This isn't real data; it's just an example.

	Factor A	*Crime*
February	.50 million	50,000
March	.75 million	60,000
April	1.00 million	70,000
May	2.00 million	140,000
June	3.00 million	200,000

I asked: *What conclusion could someone draw who was eager to find a cause-and-effect relationship?* The obvious response is that Factor A causes crime.

I asked: *Suppose it turns out that the mysterious Factor A was only ice cream sales? Why did it look as if there could be a relationship between ice cream sales and crime?* The best answer here is that they are both related to the warmer weather.

Often scientists have to settle for less than an answer to why. Sometimes they have to settle for a lot of information about what is occurring.

I asked: *What do scientists do about the difficulty of finding out why things occur?* I explained that they adopt a very cautious attitude toward any possible explanation. No matter how plausible something sounds or how many people believe it, they do not accept it unless it is proven by experiment. For example, investigators studying yellow fever exposed themselves and volunteers to bites of particular mosquitos that had been feeding on yellow fever victims in order to prove that mosquito bites could spread the disease. They also had volunteers sleep on bedding from yellow fever victims and use blankets from yellow fever victims to show that doing these things did not spread the disease (de Kruif, 1926).

I asked: *What if someone decided to be as cautious as a scientist in everyday life and always be very cautious about thinking he or she knows why something happened? In what kinds of circumstances would this caution be good? In what kinds of circumstances would it be bad?* Sometimes people jump to conclusions and blame somebody else for something bad that happened — it would be good to be cautious about that. Being cautious would lead to feeling less anger and might save a possibly constructive relationship.

Sometimes people know something is bad for their health, but instead of accepting this information and changing their diet to make it healthier, they take a very skeptical position and say they don't know exactly how bad it is or why it's bad for their health. In this case, it would be healthier to be less skeptical and decide "if it's bad for me I'll stop doing it and worry about the details later."

26

Workshop:
Some Things Make Me Nervous

I asked: *Before I came down here today, I considered two titles for this workshop, "Some things make me nervous" and "Some things make you nervous." The reason I did that is that some people say that it is easier to see if someone else is nervous, and sometimes we can be nervous about something without realizing it. Do you think this is true?* The group responded, yes, sometimes we feel nervous and don't realize it.

I asked: *What is good about feeling nervous?* Group responses included:

it shows that you're sensitive, aware, and caring;

it can help you improve your performance; and

it can help you avoid danger, and learn safety rules.

I then asked: *What is bad about feeling nervous?* They responded that

it's painful;

it takes a lot of energy;

it can cause panic, accidents, or bad decisions;

sometimes people are afraid of things that aren't really dangerous;

sometimes people are so afraid of certain things that they restrict their lives to
the point that it isn't good for their mental health; and

sometimes people feel silly because other people can tell that they feel
nervous.

I asked: *What are the signs that we feel nervous about something?* The
group named symptoms including:

heart rate, shakiness;
worrying;
sweaty palms, biting nails;
breathing heavily;
walking the floor;
fearful thoughts;
avoiding things;
making excuses; and
feeling relieved when something is over.

I asked: *How can feelings of nervousness be overcome?* The group
suggested distraction, medication, information, skill-building, relaxation, and humor.

At this point I would give a demonstration of how to think about feelings of nervousness in such a way as to help overcome them. Using the
basic principle of rational emotive behavior therapy — that it is your
thoughts about an event that affect your feelings — I set up a chart on the
blackboard for discussing someone's feelings of nervousness about
something. I had three columns on the blackboard — Event, Thoughts,
and Feelings.

One group member confided that he felt afraid to go on group trips. He
was afraid he might have a car accident. It turned out to be a really good
example, because it showed the group that everyone's fears are unique
and that, when you look carefully at your own fears, they may be different from what you thought. He said his fear about an accident had very
little to do with being injured. He was afraid he would get stranded
somewhere for a few hours and have to make small talk for all that time.
He would feel so guilty for wasting so much time and think he should
have known better than to go on the trip. He could see that thinking "I
should have known better" and "I shouldn't waste time" made him feel
very guilty and upset. We discussed ways that he could try to feel less
guilty about wasting time. He could keep in mind that everyone wasted
time unintentionally because it isn't always possible to know the most
productive way to spend time. He focused on thinking "I would like to be

doing something more useful" rather than "I should be doing something more useful." The next week he reported that he had gone on an outing for the first time in a long time and had enjoyed it.

In other groups, I also got good examples about fears of going on a ferris wheel or fears of people being critical, staring, and thinking the group member wasn't normal.

I think the format of having a factual discussion about feelings of nervousness first enabled the group to feel comfortable about bringing up personal examples, because they knew exactly the kind of common sense framework in which the examples were going to be handled.

I asked: *What do bats and bankruptcy have in common?* The group guessed that both were always moving, wanted all they could get, and were not responsible. The actual answer is that they are both things that some people fear. This joke was a way of introducing the idea that fears, although they may sound rational, have an irrational component. Different people are afraid of completely different things, and what scares one person, even though it may be something that is a potential danger to everyone, doesn't scare another person.

I shared with the group a poem called "Whatif" by Shel Silverstein (1981), in which a lot of fears are listed. The group enjoyed composing their own list of fears, as follows:

What if I fail?

What if my oculomotor coordination failed?

What if I run into so-and-so and I don't want to see them?

What if somebody keeps talking to me and won't stop?

What if somebody calls me on the telephone?

What if my alarm clock doesn't go off?

What if they fire me?

What if I never find a job?

What if I drown in the swimming pool?

What if the bank rejects my loan?

What if the rent is raised?

What if I can't pay my bills?

What if it rains on the picnic?

27

Workshop:
What if People Can't
Understand Me?

I asked: *What kinds of things do people find hard to understand?* The group answered: almost anything, anything unusual, and anything complicated.

I asked: *Should I be able to explain myself to anybody?* The group responded that it would be very hard, and the person would have to be willing, able, and have time.

I asked: *Why is it hard for people to understand one another?* The group came up with quite a long list for this one. They suggested:

moods;

different education, age, sex, culture, language, and personality;

different "wavelengths;"

different interests;

different modes of communication;

easily hurt feelings;

sometimes we forget that explanations are necessary or feel silly about having to explain;

people have limited understanding, time, patience, and experience;

many things are very complicated;

people may expect things to be clear right away;

negative attitude; and
people might not want to listen.

Reasons for not listening included:

listening is an effort,
preoccupation with something else,
wanting to talk,
believing something different,
being committed to something different, or
not having time.

I asked: *How can I make myself more understandable?* Suggestions included:

practice;
keep things simple;
choose someone who likes to listen or has time;
look for something in common;
begin at the beginning;
ask people if they want to hear the short version, the long version, or the medium version;
use an interpreter;
tell a little bit at a time, like a teacher;
talk slowly and loudly enough; and
pick a good time.

I asked: *Is it always important to be understood?* The group decided that it was pleasant but not necessary. I emphasized that if they realize they don't have to be understood, they may feel more patient about seeking understanding, and may be able to persist until they find it.

28

Workshop:
What Really Counts?

I asked: *What qualities are good to have for playing volleyball?* The group responded that a good player would be tall, have lots of energy, be coordinated, be alert, be a good sport, be a good team player, be agile, have strength, and have endurance.

Then I asked: *What counts in volleyball?* In volleyball only points count.

I asked: *What qualities are good to have to play pick-up sticks?* For this game a player must be slow and careful.

Then I asked: *What counts in a game of pick-up sticks?* In pick-up sticks, how many sticks you can pick up is all that counts.

Finally, I asked: *How is real life fuller and more complicated than games?* The group responded:

You don't have to play competitively.
You can get help with your goals.
You can change goals as you go along.
More things count.
You can say "I'm sorry."
You can discuss.

Feelings change and you can laugh later at something that seemed bad at the
    time.

Different kinds of things can count as successful.

Different people count different things.

Consequences are real.

Rules are unclear.

The "weak" are as important as the "strong."

29

Workshop: Patience

I stated: *The word "patience" sounds a little old-fashioned today. We have gadgets to do everything faster, computers, fast food, and so on. Is patience still needed or not?*

The group agreed that there are still a lot of things we have to wait for. Because of our expectation that things in the modern world will go quickly, it may be especially hard to deal with situations that require patience.

I told a couple of stories about the idea that everybody in the modern world thinks things should be done as quickly as possible. I told how, a number of years ago, I still had a rotary phone. Somebody saw it and laughed very hard because she thought that everybody had a touch tone phone. I told the joke about the motorist waiting at an intersection after the light had changed while a little old lady very slowly finished crossing the street. The driver in back of him kept honking his horn until finally the motorist got out of his car, handed his car keys to the driver in back of him and said, "O.K. You run her over."

I asked: *What situations require patience?* The group suggested waiting in line and waiting for somebody.

I asked: *Why is it so hard to be patient?* The group stated it was hard to visualize or understand why things take so much time.

We talked about how some situations just can't be hurried, like growing a plant. Sometimes we don't know why something is taking so long,

and after failing to make it go faster, it is easier to assume it is like waiting for some mysterious growth process rather than to assume it is something that we should know how to push faster.

Using a rational emotive behavioral format, we listed different situations requiring patience and the kinds of thoughts that help us feel calmer
versus the kinds of thoughts that make us feel more impatient.

We talked about how, when waiting in line, instead of thinking "they
should move faster," it was a good time to tune out and use your imagination and think about something enjoyable. I gave an example from
Catch-22 (Heller, 1955) of a character with an unusual attitude. He actually chose to do a boring activity because he wanted his life to feel as if it
were lasting longer. Waiting in line is an opportunity to cultivate a
leisurely attitude.

The situation of waiting for somebody evoked a lot of feelings. People
often had the thought, "What if they forgot about meeting me because
they don't care about it?"

One group member brought up feelings of impatience about the state
of world politics. He thought, "I have to do something about this," and he
felt frantic. He felt better when he remembered that certain things had
changed for the better over long periods of time.

I asked: *What helps to develop patience?* The group's list included:

Develop imagination.
Develop a sense of commitment.
Take an interest in the obstacles, not just the final result.
Take pride in growing more patient.
Don't expect too much too soon.

Then I asked: *What are the advantages of developing patience?*
Feeling better and becoming better able to do important future-oriented
things like saving money and working on self-improvement projects
were the group's answers.

30

Workshop:
Honesty

I picked a time near Washington's birthday to do this topic and had a sketch of a fallen cherry tree on the easel pad along with the title of the workshop.

I asked: *Why are people sometimes not honest, even when they'd like to be?* I explained that I wasn't talking about crimes, just about everyday behavior. The group responded that people

are afraid to say they don't know,

are worried about opposition,

don't want to disappoint people,

don't want to take on too much responsibility,

are not satisfied with the truth,

think no one else is honest,

decide it is not convenient,

don't think all the way ahead, and

are not willing to stand alone.

The group surprised me with the long list of reasons for not being honest and with their enthusiasm for this topic. Somewhere in the middle of this discussion, I told them the story of the Emperor's New Clothes (Anderson, 1949), which, to my surprise, several of them were unfamiliar with. I also told them about Asch's findings that, if research subjects are asked to make judgments about length, they can be influenced to give the wrong answer by putting them in a group where they hear everyone else give the wrong answer (Hilgard, Atkinson, & Atkinson, 1975).

I asked: *What are the advantages of honesty?* The group suggested

It puts friendships on a firmer foundation.
Knowledge grows if you keep an open mind, ask questions, and look things up when you don't know.
It brings more peace of mind.
It gives you a better reputation.

I asked: *What encourages others to talk honestly to you?* The group decided that by being honest with them and not reacting negatively to hearing the truth, others could be encouraged to be honest.

The group reacted very positively to this topic. I think it is a very important subject for people with serious mental illnesses, because they often feel intimidated about their level of functioning. Because they imagine that others are perfect, they don't reveal their flaws and don't hear about the flaws of others, so they go on thinking that the others are perfect.

31

General Comments about the Workshops in the Residential Care Settings

Some of the residents in these settings were drawn to these topics and conversations and often felt relief from their loneliness. Some fairly withdrawn residents attended approximately once a month even though the workshops were given more often. Because the workshop topics were based upon sound cognitive principles, I think that the temporary relief from loneliness that these residents experienced justified the existence of the group. In medicine, we accept the value of many treatments whose purpose is simply to alleviate pain, but somehow, in psychiatry, we often feel that everything must be justified in terms of proven long-term benefits. Although clinical recovery is a gradual process, there are some elements of social recovery — such as living independently or becoming employed — that occur all at once when opportunities become available. Clinical recovery has to be maintained long enough for these opportunities to occur. Any activity that helps the individual to maintain wellness can, thus, be critical to his or her eventually achieving a social recovery.

References

Abelson, R. P. (1973). The structure of belief systems. In R. C. Shank & K. M. Colby (Eds.), *Computer models of thought and language* (pp. 287–339). San Francisco, CA: W. H. Freeman.

American Psychiatric Association. (1994). *Diagnostic and Statistical Manual of Mental Disorders,* 4th ed. (p. xxiv). Washington, DC: American Psychiatric Press.

Anderson, H. C. (1949). *The emperor's new clothes.* Boston: Houghton Mifflin.

Barsh, A. L., & Jackson, M. (1996). Information needs of special populations: Serving people with mental illnesses using computer aided instruction in a multimedia library for outpatients. *The Reference Librarian, 25* (53).

Beers, C. W. (1953). *A mind that found itself: An autobiography,* 5th ed. (p. 30). New York: Doubleday.

Bellack, A. S., & Mueser, K. T. (1993). Psychosocial treatment for schizophrenia. *Schizophrenia Bulletin, 19,* 317–336.

Briggs Myers, I., & Myers, P. B. (1980). *Gifts differing.* Palo Alto, CA: Consulting Psychologists Press.

Chinn, C. A., & Brewer, W. F. (1993). The role of anomalous data in knowledge acquisition: A theoretical framework and implications for science instruction. *Review of Educational Research, 63*(1), 1–49.

de Kruif, P. (1926). *Microbe hunters* (pp. 286–307). New York: Harcourt Brace Jovanovich.

Eisel, D. D., & Reddig, J. S. (Eds.). (1981). *Dictionary of contemporary quotations* (p. 40). U.S.A.: John Gordon Burke.

Ellis, A. (1994). Post-traumatic stress disorder (PTSD): A rational emotive behavioral theory. *Journal of Rational-Emotive & Cognitive-Behavior Therapy, 12*(1), 3–25.

____. (1993). Changing rational-emotive therapy (RET) to rational emotive behavior therapy (REBT). *The Behavior Therapist, 16*(10), 257–258.

____. (1962). *Reason and emotion in psychotherapy* (pp. 286, 287). Secaucus, NJ: Citadel.

Ellis, A., & Harper, R. A. (1975). *A new guide to rational living.* North Hollywood, CA: Wilshire.

Freud, S. (1967). *The interpretation of dreams* (p. 482). New York: Avon. (Original work published 1899).

Gerbner, G., Morgan, M., & Signorielli, N. (1982). Programing health portrayals: What viewers see, say, and do. In D. Pearl, L. Bouthilet & J. Lazar (Eds.), *Television and behavior: Ten years of scientific progress and implications for the eighties,* Vol. 2 (pp. 291–307). Rockville, MD: U.S. Department of Health and Human Services.

Greist, J. H., Gustafson, D. H., Stauss, F. F., Rowse, G. L., Laughren, T. P., & Chiles, J. A. (1973). A computer interview for suicide risk prediction. *American Journal of Psychiatry, 130,* 1327–1332.

Greist, J. H., Klein, M. H., & VanCura, L. J. (1973). A computer interview for psychiatric patient target symptoms. *Archives of General Psychiatry, 29,* 247–253.

Harless, W. (1986). An interactive videodisc drama: The case of Frank Hall. *Journal of Computer-Based Instruction, 13*(4), 113–116.

Heller, J. (1955). *Catch-22* (pp. 39–40). New York: Dell.

Henderson, J. V., & Galper, A. R. (1987). Advanced combat trauma life support. Interactive video to teach combat trauma care management. Presentation at the Annual Nebraska Videodisc Symposium, October 7.

Hilgard, E. R., Atkinson, R. C., & Atkinson, R. L. (1975). *Introduction to psychology,* 6th ed. (pp. 551–552). New York: Harcourt Brace Jovanovich.

Kingdon, D. G., & Turkington, D. (1994). *Cognitive-behavioral therapy of schizophrenia* (pp. 82–92, 127–188). New York: Guilford.

Liberman, R. P., & Corrigan, P. W. (1993). Designing new psychosocial treatments for schizophrenia. *Psychiatry, 56,* 238–249.

Liberman, R. P., Mueser, K. T., Wallace, C. J., Jacobs, H. E., Eckman, T., & Massel, H. K. (1986). Training skills in the psychiatrically disabled: Learning coping and competence. *Schizophrenia Bulletin, 12,* 631–647.

Meichenbaum, D. (1994). *A clinical handbook/practical therapist manual for assessing and treating adults with post-traumatic stress disorder (PTSD)* (pp. 349–359). Waterloo, Ontario: Institute Press.

Olevitch, B. A., & Hagan, B. J. (1994). "How to Get Out and Stay Out": An interactive videodisc simulation for psychiatric wellness education. *Computers in Human Services, 11,* 177–188.

____. (1991). An interactive videodisc as a tool in the rehabilitation of the chronically mentally ill: A preliminary investigation. *Computers in Human Behavior, 7,* 57–73.

____. (1989). "How to Get Out and Stay Out": An educational videodisc for the chronically mentally ill. *Computers in Human Services, 5*(3/4), 57–69.

Propst, L. R., Ostrom, R., Watkins, P., Dean, T., & Mashburn, D. (1992). Comparative efficacy of religious and nonreligious cognitive-behavioral therapy for the treatment of clinical depression in religious individuals. *Journal of Consulting and Clinical Psychology, 60,* 94–103.

Resick, P. A., & Schnicke, M. K. (1993). *Cognitive processing therapy for rape victims: A treatment manual* (pp. 9–21). Newbury Park, CA: Sage.

Reus, V. I., Weingartner, H., & Post, R. M. (1979). Clinical implications of state-dependent learning. *American Journal of Psychiatry, 136,* 927–931.

Scheff, T. (1966). *Being mentally ill: A sociological theory* (p. 81). Chicago: Aldine.

Scott, J., Byers, S., & Turkington, D. (1993). The chronic patient. In J. H. Wright, M. E. Thase, A. T. Beck, & J. W. Ludgate (eds.), *Cognitive therapy with inpatients: Developing a cognitive milieu* (pp. 357–390). New York: Guilford.

Selmi, P. M., Klein, M. H., Greist, J. H., Johnson, J. H., & Harris, W. G. (1982). An investigation of computer-assisted cognitive-behavior therapy in the treatment of depression. *Behavior Research Methods & Instrumentation, 14*(2), 181–185.

Silverstein, S. (1981). *A light in the attic* (p. 90). New York: Harper & Row.

Simons, A. D., Murphy, G. E., Levine, J. L., & Wetzel, R. D. (1986). Cognitive therapy and pharmacotherapy for depression: sustained improvement over one year. *Archives of General Psychiatry, 43,* 43–48.

Singer, J. L. (1974). *Imagery and daydream methods in psychotherapy and behavior modification* (pp. 1–18). New York: Academic Press.

Thase, M. E., & Beck, A. T. (1993). Overview of cognitive therapy. In J. H. Wright, M. E. Thase, A. T. Beck, & J. W. Ludgate (eds.), *Cognitive therapy with inpatients: Developing a cognitive milieu* (pp. 3–34). New York: Guilford.

Turner, B. A. (1991, Winter). Somatic vs. social therapy: Which is more effective? *Missouri Mental Health Consumer (MMHCN) Networker, 3*(1), 4–5.

Wright, J. H., Thase, M. E., Beck, A. T., & Ludgate, J. W. (1993). *Cognitive therapy with inpatients: Developing a cognitive milieu.* New York: Guilford.

Zubin, J. (1980). Chronic schizophrenia from the standpoint of vulnerability. In C. Baxter and T. Melnechuk (Eds.), *Perspectives in Schizophrenia Research.* (pp. 269–294). New York: Raven.

Zubin, J., & Spring, B. (1977). Vulnerability — A new view of schizophrenia. *Journal of Abnormal Psychology, 86,* 103–126.

Zubin, J., Steinhauer, S. R., Day, R., & van Kammen, D. P. (1985). Schizophrenia at the crossroads: A blueprint for the 80s. *Comprehensive Psychiatry, 26,* 217–240.

Index

ABOUT THE AUTHOR

BARBARA A. OLEVITCH is Director of the Psychiatric Wellness Education Program in St. Louis, Missouri. Olevitch received her Ph.D. in Clinical Psychology from Yale University and has worked extensively with the mentally ill.